# ITA WEGMAN
## AND
# ANTHROPOSOPHY

# ITA WEGMAN
## AND
# ANTHROPOSOPHY

*A Conversation with Emanuel Zeylmans*

WOLFGANG WEIRAUCH

SteinerBooks
2012

*The publisher wishes to acknowledge the support of **Joanna Arripol**, without whom publication of this translation would not have been possible.*

SteinerBooks
610 Main Street, Great Barrington, MA 01230
www.steinerbooks.org

Translated by Matthew Barton.

Originally published in German as *Ita Wegman und die Anthroposophie: Ein Gesprach mit Emanuel Zeylmans* by Flensburger Hefte Verlag, 1996.

ISBN 978-1-62148-012-9
ISBN 978-1-62148-024-2 (eBook)

Library of Congress Cataloging-in-Publication Data is available.

# CONTENTS

# PREFACE

In most human communities there is a scapegoat who is blamed for the mistakes, failures, weaknesses, and unacknowledged potential for the conflict of others. Rather than looking in the mirror of self-knowledge, people tend to take their agression out on someone else.

In the first decades after the 1923 Christmas Foundation Meeting, Ita Wegman, Rudolf Steiner's closest collaborator in the last years of his life, became the whipping stick of the Anthroposophical Society. Criticism of her did not fall silent at her death, but was repeatedly kept alive by prejudice and the untruths about her that circulated. This gave rise to a conflagration whose smog obscured a clear and unprejudiced view of Wegman for decades. Even well-meaning and unpartisan people found it difficult in the past to see through this smokescreen, since almost all the available information was one-sided and there was no biography about Wegman and her work at Steiner's side. This gap was filled by Emanuel Zeylmans in his three-volume, documented biography.

Appearing in 1990 and 1992 these three volumes make up one of the largest-scale, most painstaking pieces of literature and research to come out of the anthroposophical movement. Emanuel Zeylmans took twelve years gathering material for his Wegman biography, alongside his work as a Christian Community priest. He started from total chaos: there were a hundred undated notebooks, two thousand manuscript pages and six thousand of Wegman's letters to struggle through. To get some order and system in this confusion, Zeylmas had to retreat from the world for many weeks, for his daily work would have made it very hard to fit together all the jigsaw pieces of Wegman's literary estate into a single, chronologically ordered whole.

During these twelve years of work, which at times took him to the very limits of endurance, Zeylmans also came upon esoteric material that was under a taboo of silence—the verses and mantras which Steiner gave Wegman. An immeasurable treasure was thus opened to him, which offered a glimpse into the significance of Wegman and Steiner's collaboration over many incarnations—from the Ephesus Mysteries to the present day.

The help of Friedrich Kröner, as editor, in giving form to the whole, was decisive in preparing the Wegman documentation. Both also succeeded in obtaining publication rights for the exchange of letters between Wegman and Steiner, from the places which—because of the old conflicts—still would not enter into dialogue with one another.

This book is no second biography of Ita Wegman, but focuses on Emanuel Zeylmans' life and chief work. Here you will read how his interesting and eventful life led him, as though by the hand of destiny, to compile the three volumes of *Who Was Ita Wegman?* The following interview bears witness to the way in which we can, despite all circuitous routes, despair, and backward steps, complete our life's work, and how, on the way to our goal, we can work through all the opposition and hindrances that block our path.

# I

# INTRODUCTORY

*This book is based on long and intense conversations which I had with Emanuel Zeylmans at his house in Ersrode near Kassel. The following text, which Emanuel Zeylmans wrote as an introduction to the first volume of his Ita Wegman biography, may serve as an introduction to our theme. It gives a good overview of Wegman's life, and her work on behalf of anthroposophy at Rudolf Steiner's side; and briefly sets out the problematic situation confronting Emanuel Zeylmans when he undertook his documented study.*

Rudolf Steiner and the anthroposophy which he developed did not become internationally known during his lifetime. Since then the anthroposophical movement has become active in every continent and, with the circulation of his writings and the application of anthroposophy to practical fields such as Waldorf education, biodynamic agriculture, art (e.g., eurythmy), as well as in science and theology, it has become more widely recognized. This has led to a growing interest in the origins of the anthroposophical movement, its history, and the lives of the anthroposophical pioneers—among whom is Ita Wegman.

She was born in Java, Indonesia, on February 22, 1876, studied medicine in Zurich from 1906 to 1911, and in 1921 founded a clinic in Arlesheim, Switzerland. For a few years she engaged in intensive collaboration with Rudolf Steiner (1861-1925), and up to 1925 was a member of the Vorstand, or executive council of the Anthroposophical Society. At Steiner's request she took over direction of the newly-founded Medical Section of the School for Spiritual Science at the end of 1923. From then on until her death on March 4, 1943 in Arlesheim, she worked to develop the new medical movement and anthroposophical curative education.

Ita Wegman in Zurich (circa 1907)

Her development, life, and work have until now been recorded only in some reminiscences by her contemporaries and a few articles. Until now there was no biography. But since she had a large circle of patients and colleagues, undertook many trips abroad, and was an open and energetic person, she lived on in the memories of many people after her death.

Beside her collaboration on Steiner's last book, *Fundamentals of Therapy*, Ita Wegman's written work is confined to a large number of articles for periodicals originating mainly between 1925 and 1932. She left no biographical material apart from a few notes.

In contrast to many other prominent anthroposophists she rarely gave lectures, putting her energies instead into human encounters and her work: she set up a nursing school; helped found medical centers in Berlin, London, and Paris; was involved in developing curative education homes; started the periodical

*Natura* (1926-1940); and initiated off-shoots of her clinic in Figino, Tirol, and Ascona.

As long as this was still possible, she devoted her well-developed organizational talent chiefly to research work and training doctors and medical students. Wherever she could, she helped develop anthroposophical remedies and make them known. In doing this she drew on two gifts which no doubt moved Rudolf Steiner to hand over leadership of the Medical Section at the Goetheanum to her: firstly, her fresh, open, heart-warming nature that was a lasting inspiration to many of her colleagues; and secondly, a caring way with doctors, nurses, and curative teachers, which made them feel affirmed and supported in their profession and plans.

Opposition to her and her activities developed at an early stage in some circles of the Anthroposophical Society—and not, as is often assumed, only after Steiner's death. But it was not until 1925 that more vocal complaints were raised against her, in connection with her anthroposophical schooling work in the First Class, a course of esoteric instruction at the School for Spiritual Science. Her *To the Members* articles in the newsletter *What is Happening in the Anthroposophical Society*, also met with resistance in certain quarters when they were published in 1925. She was accused of power-lust and unwarranted "occult" behavior; and also of misusing hints Rudolf Steiner made about a connection between them in former incarnations. These reproaches led to members dividing into different camps, and, in 1935, to Wegman's expulsion from the Anthroposophical Society, along with several thousand other members.

The complaints against her have never been fully cleared up—they relate in a particular way to Ita Wegman and her destiny, and should be distinguished from other differences of opinion between anthroposophists at the time. The discussions and arguments that took place were not always based on facts, and they still continue to this day. Clarification is made difficult by the fact that one still cannot gain access to some archives; and there were other circumstances, too, which hampered fruitful biographical work. So far there has been no complete overview of her life and work, so that no real assessment could be made of the validity of such complaints. In addition, the conflicts were dramatized to an extent that did not accord with historical reality. The mood of great veneration, even idolization of her which some of her colleagues and contemporaries displayed, had, according to her own account, a still more inhibiting effect on her than the conflicts in the Society.

Meeting Rudolf Steiner was decisive for Ita Wegman's life. She first met him in Berlin in 1902, but did not become one with his aims until 1923. For about two years, until he fell ill in the autumn of 1924, their collaboration was extraordinarily intense. But from the moment her Clinical-Therapeutic Institute was founded in the summer of 1921, Rudolf Steiner had begun to attend her practice from time to time to give advice. After a short while his visits increased greatly. This collaboration enabled him to involve Ita Wegman as co-author of the book *Fundamentals of Therapy*.

When Steiner decided to refound the Anthroposophical Society at the end of 1923, and to take over the office of chairman himself, he invited her to join the Vorstand, and insisted that she make her Clinic an integral part of the Society. This meant that, from 1925 onwards, the Clinical-Therapeutic Institute became a section, or branch, of the General Anthroposophical Society until it was again released from this association in 1931.

Thus, Ita Wegman witnessed Rudolf Steiner's last years from the closest proximity. She accompanied him on his many lecture tours and, as Vorstand secretary, relieved him of much work. He involved her in his esoteric research work, and a friendship between them began which was of decisive importance for the further course of her life.

Within the First Class, which had arisen in 1924 at her instigation, he gave her a leading position of responsibility, which she endeavored to sustain until her death. In this last period, until he fell ill, Rudolf Steiner was able to give vital indications for the structure of the Medical Section. As his doctor and nurse, Wegman looked after him through his illness.

Ita Wegman's literary estate and many other contemporary accounts provide better documentation of the years between 1925

Ita Wegman in Arnheim (July 1924)

and 1943 than of the preceding period. She was forty-nine years old when Rudolf Steiner died. In the following years she underwent great changes in character and spiritual constitution. Her contemporaries may not at first have seen any outward signs of this. Although she was one of the longest-standing members, she was regarded as something of a newcomer in the changed working conditions of anthroposophical life after the 1923 Christmas Foundation Meeting. To many she seemed undeserving of the close collaboration she enjoyed with Rudolf Steiner. In these few years he expressly drew her into the foreground of his work.

She took on this role with innate self-composure. Since her choleric temperament could erupt without warning, and her handling of human relationships sometimes seemed tactless, she soon made enemies. Her unclear way of expressing herself often led to misunderstandings. This very spontaneous woman probably did not easily acknowledge that circumstances in a fast-growing international movement required a certain degree of tact and restraint in its leaders. She relied on the good will of those around her, which was not present in all her fellow human beings — in fact only in those who knew her and wished to collaborate with her. For them she was a warm-hearted, supportive partner for life.

Her life was many-faceted and eventful, not only because of her friendship with Steiner. She worked day and night to further her high aims, and achieved a great deal. Despite much change and transformation, her life is marked by the sort of consistency and continuity that cries out for a biography. Words she spoke in her last days may stand over this attempt to provide one as a continual reminder: she asked that nothing should be said about her at her funeral except that she would always serve Rudolf Steiner, and that he had been her only personal teacher.

Now, half a century later, in writing a book about her and remembering these words of hers, one has to ask whether one can find the right way of expressing things, for *"What is the true language for what has truly been?"* (Peter Handke). In her deeds and sufferings Ita Wegman took part in a transformation of the world. In trying to do justice to her life therefore, a biographical description will surely not confine itself to her individual importance, but will also examine the value of her life's goals. This is what she herself would wish.

Over and above a factual and consistent account of actions and events, this necessitates a certain harmony, too, between biographical description and the underlying impulses at work in Ita Wegman's life. Experience teaches us that the essential is also what is fruitful. So if the biographer wishes to stay true to his subject, he must cast his gaze on all that is positive. He must not overlook the shadow side, but nor must he be seduced by it. Thus I have attempted to observe this life story without prejudice but not uncritically, for *"a problem a person thinks he has solved denies him the chance of seeing a thousand things clearly which belong in the realm of this problem."*

## *A spider's web of strange emotions*

**Wolfgang Weirauch:** Ita Wegman was one of the anthroposophical movement's most outstanding personalities at the beginning of the last century. Despite this she practically vanished from memory in following decades. What was the situation regarding Ita Wegman when you started work on your three-volume biography in 1980? What importance was ascribed to her within the anthroposophical movement?

**Emanuel Zeylmans:** As I pondered the possibility of writing a biography of Ita Wegman in 1980, read reminiscences of her and spoke to people about her, I soon got the feeling of being caught up in a kind of spider's web. This resulted from verbal comments and condemnations I heard about Ita Wegman. There was something strange and uneasy connected with this theme, and the subject of Ita Wegman was enveloped in a sort of taboo.

I often felt this, for instance, when visiting a lady in Basel whom I knew, with whom I had always had the friendliest conversations up until then. But when I told her that I was researching into Ita Wegman, this anthroposophical lady exploded in anger. It was very strange. She was almost in a frenzy. She had not even known Ita Wegman. I then tried to discover the reason for this outbreak, and met an extraordinary swell of emotions. Over the years I have met other people who reacted in a similar way. Others were more self-controlled, but in general views were extremely turbulent. I gradually came to see that these emotional reactions and misjudgments belong to Ita Wegman's biography. It is an aspect of Ita Wegman's biography that, at the mere mention of her name, people still lose control fifty years after her death, and explode in anger.

Of course things were different at the Ita Wegman Clinic in Arlesheim, for her memory still lives on there as the founder and first doctor, with whom Rudolf Steiner initiated anthroposophical medicine. And in Holland too, my own country, views about Ita Wegman are much more varied. There is a positive mood about her there.

So quite soon after getting involved with this Wegman theme I noticed that strange, sweeping judgments held sway in regard to her, that a number of negative anecdotes had been passed on through decades, and that many people were simply uninterested in her.

Rudolf Steiner

### *Rudolf Steiner — my life's inspiration*

**W W**: Who was Rudolf Steiner (1861-1925) and what importance does he have for you?

**Emanuel Zeylmans**: My picture of Rudolf Steiner has in recent years been largely determined by my study of his biography, *The Course of My Life (Autobiography: Chapters in the Course of My Life 1861-1907)*. I see Rudolf Steiner as my life's inspiration, and this has been so for the past 38 years. As I became aware of his importance I gave increasing attention to him. Particularly through working on the Ita Wegman biography I deepened my involvement and interest in Rudolf Steiner.

Since then I have been continually and vividly aware of his importance. For me he is one of the few people of our times who has developed new and fruitful ideas about life; and whose path one can follow oneself to understand how he came to these ideas. One can learn how to think fruitfully from Rudolf Steiner.

Marie Steiner

## Marie Steiner

**WW:** Who was Marie Steiner (1867-1948, member of the General Anthroposophical Society's founding Vorstand and leader of the Section for Dramatic and Musical Arts), and what importance does she have for you?

**Emanuel Zeylmans:** In relation to anthroposophy and my own profession she is not someone who particularly interests me. Of course I have often encountered her work, above all as publisher of Rudolf Steiner's books. Naturally I have also tried to get to know as much as possible about her life. In doing so I observed that she was of great importance to Rudolf Steiner between 1902 and 1920. Thus, I perceive her importance when I examine Rudolf Steiner's activity during this time. She enabled him to grasp hold of his mission.

Marie Steiner also always took care to protect Rudolf Steiner from undue pressure from other people close to him. It has always surprised me that he coped with this mood of veneration from his followers. One can probably only explain this by seeing the part Marie Steiner played. She had the demeanor and attitude of soul rigorous enough to keep people away from him. She was also very gifted at organizing things and could protect him. In his book *Gelebte Erwartung* (Living in expectation) (Stuttgart, 1979), Ernst Lehrs records an anecdote from a meeting at which Rudolf Steiner seemed "elsewhere," because he was observing something spiritually:

> As he sat there before us he seemed outwardly tired. The fact that he was not was apparent at the beginning of the meeting when he addressed one of the questions we had put to him [...], and at the first lecture of the course which he gave immediately afterwards. Later I learned, from friends who had seen him look like this on numerous previous occasions, that this had a different cause. He could appear like this physically when he elevated himself to visionary awareness, for instance so as to be able to offer to someone sitting before him some advice that was right for him. This could also happen in the middle of discussions with others, when he was called for a short time into the spiritual realm. Sometimes it even looked as though he had nodded off. Wherever possible Frau Dr. Steiner then served him by talking vivaciously to those present—a gift she did not lack—and at the same time bending unobtrusively in front of him, thus concealing him from others' view until he returned.

For me this is a wonderful image of Marie Steiner's mission!

## *Ita Wegman*

**WW:** Who was Ita Wegman (1876-1943, member of the General Anthroposophical Society's founding Vorstand and leader of the Medical Section) and what importance does she have for you?

**Emanuel Zeylmans:** First and foremost is the health of her soul, which becomes obvious when one compares her with other

Ita Wegman (1925)

prominent anthroposophists. She also had a healthy common sense, was trusting of and inspiring to her fellow human beings— a gift that is nowadays rather in decline. Nowadays many people tend to be weak and no longer free in their relations with others. But Ita Wegman had a healthy, natural relationship with the world around her.

However I would like to add that I have been against making comparisons between people since reading Ossip Mandelstam, a Russian poet. Stalin almost succeeded in wiping him out of world history. He says that people are beings who cannot be compared with each another. But when one examines anthroposophical history—Steiner and his colleagues—one cannot really help making comparative judgments about people sometimes. So one should develop a sense for the quality of every human being. We will have to increasingly learn to distinguish people's spiritual qualities. For instance, Marie Steiner is not Joan of Arc, Ita Wegman is not Alexander the Great, nor Albert Steffen King Solomon.

Albert Steffen

So when one talks about these people, one should try to perceive their real individuality, not immediately make judgments about them. Ita Wegman's biography can enable one to develop a sense of what her individuality means, and one can distinguish this meaning from the way she expresses herself as personality. These are two different worlds.

## Albert Steffen

**W W:** Who was Albert Steffen (1884-1963), member of the General Anthroposophical Society's founding Vorstand and leader of the Humanities Section), and what importance does he have for you?

**Emanuel Zeylmans:** I do not know a great deal about Albert Steffen, and haven't even read all of his books, though I know some very fine poems by him. When I was working on the history of the Anthroposophical Society in Ita Wegman's time—1923-1943—I became familiar with Albert Steffen as editor of the *Goetheanum* periodical and the newsletter. He was in charge of editing these. Besides this, many documents have given me an impression of him as chairman of the Anthroposophical Society after Steiner's death.

I don't wish to make any judgments about Albert Steffen, but would just like to reproduce an account by Herbert Hillringhaus (1912-1987, founder and editor of *Die Kommenden* magazine). I visited him in 1970 when I wanted to start *Jonas*.

Hillringhaus had first encountered anthroposophy during the Second World War. When the war ended he went to Dornach, and what most fired his interest, above all, was the *Goetheanum* magazine. In a relatively short time he made a thorough study of the 1939-1945 issues, for he had not yet had a chance to see these. I can still see Hillringhaus' dismayed face as he told me: "Anyone who read these issues of the *Goetheanum* without knowing the Second World War had taken place, would have been none the wiser about it by the end." That is a very apt characterization of Albert Steffen as editor and writer. And perhaps it throws some light on him as Chairman of the Anthroposophical Society.

## *Who was Ita Wegman?*

**W W:** I would like to get a fuller picture from you of Ita Wegman's character. Was she really such a pleasant, sociable person, or did she have a hard edge to her?

**Emanuel Zeylmans:** One can tell from reading her letters in particular that she was an open-minded person who enjoyed social contact, who took a lot of pleasure in social interaction. Norbert Glas (a doctor, 1897-1986)—who would actually have been an ideal biographer of Ita Wegman—wrote two articles about her, which are among the best descriptions of her we have. He describes her pleasure in contact with others, her spontaneous, very open, Dutch character. But if one examines Ita Wegman's spiritual importance, one can call her a strong soul. In her soul constitution she was well and solidly incarnated, and had incredible soul forces. In the course of her doctor's practice she often spent a whole night without sleep and then worked on through the following day, without her colleagues noticing that she was at all tired.

On the other hand the anthroposophical painter Liane Collot d'Herbois described in her memoirs an outbreak of anger Ita Wegman had at the Gare du Nord in Paris. This shows us the great discrepancy in her way of relating to people: on the one hand fiery and tending to outbreaks of anger, on the other hand an extraordinarily warm and sociable person.

**WW:** Why, in his last years, did Steiner particularly seek out contact with Ita Wegman? Why did he feel particularly at ease with her?

**Emanuel Zeylmans:** He himself cast light on this riddle, for instance in the following poem he wrote to her:

> Your understanding,
> Your love and faithfulness
> Are my support.
>
> From your understanding
> I see grow
> The light that shines towards me,
>
> From your love
> I see grow
> The warmth that blesses me,
>
> From your faithfulness
> I see grow
> The air that enlivens me.

In connection with this I can relate a little anecdote. Together with Anton Gerretsen (a doctor at the Ita Wegman Clinic in Arlesheim) I visited one of Rudolf Steiner's former drivers shortly before he died at the age of 91. He had driven Steiner in 1924, and experienced him with other anthroposophists. We asked him for his impression of Rudolf Steiner. He looked at me steadily and said: "Rudolf Steiner was very lonely." When I asked him why Steiner had been so lonely, he replied: "Everyone wanted something from

Rudolf Steiner, and no one thought of doing anything for him." Ita Wegman had an eye for this, and her understanding was the light that shone for him, the warmth that blessed him and the air that enlivened him. In her presence he could probably breathe more easily, perhaps also breathe out a bit.

### *Marie Steiner is a continual presence*

**Cordula Zeylmans:** People who feel a connection with Marie Steiner naturally wonder whether she did not also give Rudolf Steiner light and warmth. Was Ita Wegman connected with what Rudolf Steiner inaugurated for the future of anthroposophy, whereas Marie Steiner stood guard over what Rudolf Steiner had already realized?

**Emanuel Zeylmans:** One continually meets such questions, as I have also found in my numerous lectures on Ita Wegman. At almost every third sentence I spoke about Ita Wegman, someone would stand up and ask whether this wasn't true also of Marie Steiner. It is symptomatic of Ita Wegman's biography that Marie Steiner continually surfaces alongside her. People continually compare them. The moment one describes a characteristic of Ita Wegman, along comes Marie Steiner again.

One can distinguish three areas of Steiner's activities: thought, word, and deed. The first realm was particularly apparent in the period up until 1900, during which he developed the ideas underlying anthroposophy. The second realm belongs to the period up to about 1919, marked by endless lecturing activity, the building of the Goetheanum (the "House of the Word"), the development of the dramatic arts and eurythmy. Marie Steiner is deeply connected with this period. Then a third area gradually comes to the fore. It is as though the world says: Everything has now been thought and said. But everything must eventually also be done. This is the beginning of the Ita Wegman era. Steiner himself coined the expression "Doing anthroposophy" in 1923.

There is a still more profound aspect, which I will speak about later.

**WW:** You have already mentioned Ita Wegman's characteristics of openness and forging links with people. This is also apparent from the large number of letters which Ita Wegman wrote, most of which you have read. What kind of impression do you get from reading them?

**Emanuel Zeylmans:** Her interest in people's destinies is particularly apparent. The real theme of her life was human destiny. Naturally this was also closely related to her professional practice in various institutes, clinics, etc.

## The four periods of Ita Wegman's life

As I gradually gained an overview of Ita Wegman's life, I noticed how she changed and developed. The first period includes roughly the first twenty-eight years of her life (up to 1904). Then came her encounter with Rudolf Steiner, and her decision to study medicine, and then to work as a doctor in Zurich up until 1920. In this phase, up until about the age of forty-four, the focus is on her intutitive nature. She must have been someone with very strong intuitive gifts, for instance in diagnosis. She did not place particular importance on this, but she was quick to sense atmospheres that others were quite unaware of.

Then comes the third period of her life, beginning with the founding of the clinic in Arlesheim in June, 1921 and ending with Rudolf Steiner's illness in September, 1924. This phase occupies just 40 months, and during it she increasingly collaborated with Rudolf Steiner—although one ought actually to say that *he* increasingly collaborated with her. This period is a unique phase in her biography, during which she underwent immense inner and outer transformation. The fourth period of her life lasts about eighteen years, and during it she lives much more consciously. This phase, up to her death in 1943, can be divided into two sections—the time up to 1934, when she was expelled from the Anthroposophical Society (although she was still officially a member of the Vorstand until 1935) and the period after this. During the first half of this fourth phase she was enormously active and conscious in relation to the outside world. In the second half of this phase she was less active outwardly, but all the more conscious in everything she undertook.

## *Her language*

**WW:** Ita Wegman did not speak fluent German. What effect did her manner of speaking have on people listening to her?

**Emanuel Zeylmans:** That is a difficult question. Many people have said that her spoken German was not very good, both in accent and grammar. She even spoke Dutch with a Malayan accent, and her English was rather poor as well. Madeleine van Deventer (1899-1983, doctor, colleague, and successor to Ita Wegman at the Clinical-Therapeutic Institute at Arlesheim) once told me that Rudolf Steiner had once said Ita Wegman was not a "person of the word." That may have been why she prepared all her addresses and lectures in written form first. For quite awhile I had about 140 of her notebooks, in which she drafted her speeches. One can see from them that she could write German well, fairly free of errors apart from a few Dutch turns of phrase. But the moment she had to express herself verbally, it became clear that she was not a gifted speaker.

There is a certain intangible quality in each person's way of speaking that goes beyond the content of what is said—something of their inner nature, that does not relate to any particular content. This element was very strong in Ita Wegman. A young doctor, Marianne Fiechter, who came to Arlesheim for the first time to attend a lecture by Ita Wegman, relates the following: Ita Wegman began her lecture, striding up and down in front of her audience; and for about five minutes Frau Fiechter, a very intelligent woman, did not understand a word. She thought to herself: "What's going on here, where on earth have I landed now?" But then she started to notice the expression on Ita Wegman's face and her powerful gestures; and although she still understood nothing she suddenly sensed that this was where she belonged.

**WW:** How did she experience this?

**Emanuel Zeylmans:** Through what worked through Wegman, despite her poor language: her real being—the expression of her spirit through her power of soul.

**WW:** Was Marianne Fiechter an exception or did other people have a similar experience of Ita Wegman's essential being when listening to her lectures? Or did Ita Wegman's poor language put people off?

**Emanuel Zeylmans:** The latter is certainly true. I can imagine that many people were prejudiced because they didn't like the way Wegman spoke. But the question is of course not what sympathies and antipathies she aroused, but what she embodied. I have heard people say that the convincing thing about Ita Wegman was what emanated from her, which also streamed out through her words.

The German language is naturally a highly developed and great cultural language. But reading a little book like the *Chymische Hochzeit Christiani Rosenkreutz (The Chemical Wedding of Christian Rosenkreutz)* for instance, one finds a very simple, transparent, almost miraculous German. If its content were not so profound, though, one would probably call it primitive. Yet when one devotes loving attention to its language, its great, profound content becomes apparent. It can be similar when someone speaks.

This was the case with Ita Wegman. Some of the clever doctors, of course, were surprised that Rudolf Steiner entrusted leadership of the Medical Section to this woman. Many of her anthroposophical contemporaries, in fact, found this very strange, a real riddle. In my view, Ita Wegman's peculiarities of speech were connected with the fact that she was so overwhelmed by ideas that she almost began to stutter. She found it difficult to clothe her impulses and ideas in language.

**Cordula Zeylmans:** People noticed that she could not express herself well in speech, and that made many of them feel embarrassed. And Germans place a good deal of importance on how people express themselves.

**WW:** But I am still not quite clear about this language problem. Did she always speak so poorly, even in her mother tongue?

Ita Wegman on the voyage to Bulgaria (1939)

Was it perhaps that it was difficult for her to learn a foreign language? If this was the case, didn't her German get better as time went by?

**Emanuel Zeylmans:** Basically she always spoke poorly. Later on she took speech formation lessons because she was a Class Reader. She did this to improve her enunciation, and it improved her accent somewhat too.

**WW:** A further peculiarity was that she sent many people to convalesce in all sorts of regions of the globe. Was this a kind of geographical therapy?

**Emanuel Zeylmans:** I asked myself the same question. What is certain is that she loved travelling. She went on trips as often as she could, simply climbed on a train, set off for Holland, then England, and back via France, etc. This travelling gave her great pleasure and was one of her great needs too. This is why she found it very difficult indeed in her last last years of life—when

## What was Ita Wegman like as a person?

### A few characteristics listed by Emanuel Zeylmans

People continually ask what Ita Wegman was like as a person. It is easier to portray her in a spoken lecture than in writing. In a lecture you have people before you who listen intently and then have an immediate experience of what you are saying. Over the years I have drawn up a whole list of characteristics which I gathered from accounts by Wegman's contemporaries. Some of these are:

Her gaze, which could take on a very dark and objective quality at a patient's bedside (Goyert and Mees);

her silences in group discussions, allowing those who otherwise remained silent to speak (Berthold);

her social awareness and colleagueship, apparent, for instance, when she filled in for a nurse who wanted to attend a performance (Stahlkopf);

her endurance at a patient's bedside (Walter and van Deventer);

her uninhibited laughter, particularly to defend herself against intellectualism in someone speaking with her (Weismann);

her interest in other people (Kruck von Poturzyn);

her practical sense of sacrifice (Einsingen);

her spartan way of life (Grosse);

her love of travelling and her capacity for endurance (Kirchner);

her sense of responsibility towards her own people (Correspondence);

"She knew what people were like" (Steiner);

her insight into the destinies of her fellow human beings (Trude Hartmann);

her gift for financial matters (Steffen);

her strength for dealing with demons (Steiner);

her wholly unconventional nature (Goebel, Collot);

her enjoyment of little plays and festivals (Sister Peggy);

her intervention on behalf of other people and children (Glas);

her interest in world politics (Sauerwein);

her concrete thinking, which made things spiritually fruitful (Bockholt).

she was in Switzerland during the Second World War—to be completely cut off from the outside world. She knew that travelling abroad refreshes people, that it enables one to experience the world, new people, other landscapes. This is why the aspect of "geographical medicine" played a great role for her. She sent people off to all regions of Europe to find healing.

**W W:** Ita Wegman was often in financial difficulties. Why did her financial problems not hinder her work?

**Emanuel Zeylmans:** That is a very profound question. In the course of my life I have known many people who had enough money yet were always beset by money worries; and others who always just had enough but never worried about money. I also know people—for instance in the Christian Community—who came to work in a parish beset by chronic lack of finances, and who managed, simply by the way they worked, to create new sources of income. Some people bring this secret power with them, and Ita Wegman had it. Perhaps it is a karmic thing?

**W W:** What was her mission in this life?

**Emanuel Zeylmans:** She probably had many missions, but the most important was connected with Rudolf Steiner's activity in the last years of his life. When you examine the early anthroposophical movement, you can distinguish different streams of people who had nothing to do with one another except their common interest in anthroposophy. In my view it was Ita Wegman's personal mission to embody the fact that anthroposophy has nothing to do with any particular streams, but is a global cultural element for all humanity.

**W W:** I like the sound of that. I could never get on with all these supposed "streams."

**Emanuel Zeylmans:** It comes from Steiner but it is extremely antiquated.

**Cordula Zeylmans:** Didn't he speak to his followers about these streams in order to help them find their place within the anthroposophical movement?

**Emanuel Zeylmans:** Yes, but that is not a reason to keep perpetuating these streams for over seventy years.

## Why Emanuel Zeylmans wrote the biography

**WW:** Why had no one previously written a biography of Ita Wegman?

**Emanuel Zeylmans:** That's what I continually asked myself too in the first few years. But over the years I noticed what a staggering amount of work is involved. Anyone who tried to undertake this would have come up against all the Society's so-called "difficulties." For this reason alone many people did not embark on it.

**WW:** Was anything at all published about Ita Wegman before 1980?

**Emanuel Zeylmans:** There were two modest memoirs. One appeared shortly after her death, the other to commemorate her centenary. Both of these were collections of reminiscences by contemporaries, written in a certain mood of reverence. Then, in 1976, came the book *Die Menschheitsaufgabe Rudolf Steiners und Ita Wegman* (Rudolf Steiner and Ita Wegman: their task for humanity) by Maragarete Kirchner-Bockholt and Erich Kirchner. In fact there is nothing new in this book about the lives of Steiner and Wegman, it is just about their former incarnations. While working on Ita Wegman's biography I also collected about a hundred articles that appeared here and there over the years. I am the sole possessor of such a collection. But all these written testimonies do not provide the outline of a biography. That's where I started from.

**WW:** When did you first get the idea that a biography of Ita Wegman ought to be written?

**Emanuel Zeylmans:** In 1979, at the request of a Swiss publisher, I wrote a biography of my father, *A Pioneer of Anthroposophy: Willem Zeylmans van Emmichoven*. This book was very well received and quickly sold out. This was my first experience of success as a biographer; and in rather an excess of high spirits I conceived the plan of writing a biography of Ita Wegman. At about the same time I got hold of the book by M. and E. Kirchner-Bockholt, and read it with some indignation because it restricts Ita Wegman to her former incarnations. The authors had not even bothered to study Ita Wegman's life. Knowing about former incarnations is only valuable inasmuch as it casts light on our current life on earth. If one does not study the present life, what value do former incarnations have (!)?

**WW:** That's sensationalism, or merely a way of satisfying curiosity.

**Emanuel Zeylmans:** Precisely. The underlying reason for their book was probably to defend her.

**Cordula Zeylmans:** But it wasn't just high spirits that made you want to write the book. You also had the feeling that it wasn't right to treat a person in the way Ita Wegman had been treated, both during her lifetime and after her death.

**Emanuel Zeylmans:** That's true. I was simply indignant that anyone could write a biography in such a way. At the time I got hold of a number of texts by Rudolf Steiner in which he speaks about Ita Wegman. These highlighted their close collaboration, but I was still left with the question of what sort of person Ita Wegman had really been. Then when I got hold of the first source materials, I began to feel I was taking on more than I could cope with, above all because there were long periods of her life that were unaccounted for. This is particularly true of her youth and the period between 1900, when she came to Europe, and 1921. Between these dates lay the Zurich period, about which I only had a collection of word-of-mouth anecdotes. It was also a long process of maturation, and for years I doubted what I was doing: I was able to write a great deal about the last years of Wegman's life, but only a few pages about the first two-thirds of it—but that wouldn't have been a biography.

The only person I could really talk to about my plans for the book was my wife Cordula. I wrote down all my ideas, doubts, questions and disappointments in various notebooks. For instance: "Today I'm sunk in depression. I now know that I won't be able to do it. I'd like to stop working and pack everything up in a box."

**WW:** Did you make these personal notes the whole time you were working on your Wegman biography?

**Emanuel Zeylmans:** I kept a diary for twelve years. It is all very sanguine, but it enabled me to objectify my work, and focus my questions.

**WW:** Did you, Frau Zeylmans, encourage your husband to write the biography when he first told you of his plan?

**Cordula Zeylmans:** Yes. Of course I had no idea of the extent of the work, but I had a deep connection with Ita Wegman's being. I also had a sense that this being of Ita Wegman would send my husband through trials and probations. That is why I kept encouraging him, for it was clear to me that anyone who writes about Ita Wegman must first make himself into a tool, an instrument. The work on this biography also came at a time that was very difficult for you, didn't it?

**Emanuel Zeylmans:** Yes, I was ill for a long time during part of the work. My wife always kept going, though I gave up completely on at least one occasion.

## II

# FROM THE LIFE OF
# EMANUEL ZEYLMANS

*Willem Zeylmans devoted himself to his ideals, even when there was no hope of fulfilling them*

**WW:** So let's start from the beginning again. Who were your parents?

**Emanuel Zeylmans:** My parents were both anthroposophists and personal students of Rudolf Steiner. My mother Ingeborg had studied eurhythmy in 1920, at the first Goetheanum. My father Willem also encountered anthroposophy in 1920, and had discussions with Rudolf Steiner. In 1923 Steiner proposed him as chairman of the Dutch Anthroposophical Society. So I grew up in a home imbued with Steiner and anthroposophy. In addition, my father had founded a clinic in Scheveningen which he called the Rudolf Steiner Clinic. This was a small anthroposophical clinic with thirty-five beds.

My parents also spiritually accompanied my work on the Ita Wegman biography after

Ingeborg Zeylmans

Willem Zeylmans

their death. I became very strongly connected to them after they died. I had intense conversations with my father, particularly in the last years of his life, so that I kept experiencing him once he had died. I only developed a direct connection with my mother after (or rather through) her death. My parents are a constant presence, and I feel continually connected to them. My mother died in 1960, my father at the end of 1961. The death of both of them gave me inner experiences of awakening.

WW: Was your relationship with your parents not so strong when you were young?

Emanuel Zeylmans: No, when I was seventeen I left my parents' home in a hurry and turned away from them altogether. In Amsterdam I opened a small second-hand bookshop with a friend, so as to be able to live. And until I was thirty-two, I wanted to have nothing to do with anthroposophy.

WW: A theme in your father's life was that many of his plans and ideas came to nothing. What significance did this have in his life?

**Emanuel Zeylmans:** My father had many great impulses and ideas. For instance he tried for years to found an institute concerned with the psychology of different nations. He twice travelled to the United States to get support for this project, but it came to nothing. My father studied the psychology of colors, and their effect on the human soul—which was also the subject of his doctor's thesis in Leipzig. Before the Second World War he founded an institute for color psychology in Holland, which actually did continue for a few years, advising various paint and carpet firms—but it did not become the kind of institute he had envisaged. He planned a book about the heavenly hierarchies, and got many people involved in the project, but the book was never written. He also had many ideas about Europe and wanted to found a kind of European Advisory Board for national and international questions.

**WW:** Those were good ideas.

**Emanuel Zeylmans:** Yes, it was all very modern and full of potential, but nothing came of these good ideas. His ideas, and their failure to take off, made a great impression on me. My father's clinic, too, was no longer the same after the Second World War. It no longer exists. The collapse of these things is part and parcel of my father's life, but he did not despair. His motto was that one should still attempt things, even if there was no hope they would be realized. There's a very nice French expression that sums this up: "Point n'est besoin d'esperer pour entreprendre, ni de réussir pour persévérer!" "You can act without having hope, and persevere without succeeding." That was the motto of William of Orange (1533-1584) who made the Netherlands into a single state.

### Youthful experiences with people who had died

**WW:** You were born in The Hague and grew up in Scheveningen where your father was director of the clinic. You had a great deal of contact there with the sick and dying. How did this affect your childhood?

**Emanuel Zeylmans:** As a small child I was of course not present when people died, but I was aware that they had died. And I often saw them laid out. The death of my grandfather made a great impression on me. He died when I was twelve. I was so affected by his death that afterward I became very ill. In the clinic, I experienced how profoundly different people are from one another. Since my father was a psychiatrist there were many mentally ill people in the clinic. This contact with mentally unstable people belongs to my biography. In the same way it is part of the picture of my life that I had numerous experiences with the dead when I was young. I dreamed about many of those who died, and sometimes I felt their close presence, so that connections with the dead were always a matter of course for me. When I became a priest, therefore, I knew how one should deal with such things.

My childhood was strongly affected by the fact that, because of the clinic, we did not have our own household. I still remember asking my mother as a young boy whether lunch was ready. She would always say: "Go and ask." Then I would skip along a long corridor, lift the roll-shutters of a lift and shout down the shaft to the kitchen: "Is lunch ready for the Zeylmans?" Shortly afterwards I could press down a pedal and then several trays would rise up out of the depths bearing food for the Zeylmans. We ate together but I never saw my mother cook once in all my childhood. My mother was a curative eurythmist in the clinic, and also gave eurythmy courses there.

### Ita Wegman gave me a radiant smile

**WW:** You met many anthroposophists at mealtimes. What impression did these people make on you?

**Emanuel Zeylmans:** I didn't realize this until my interest in Wegman began. Before that I wasn't aware that my father regularly had prominent anthroposophical visitors. But we moved quite naturally in these circles. Margarete Kirchner-Bockholt (1894–1973, a doctor) was my godmother. She carried me on her arm

Elisabeth Vreede

at my christening. Ehrenfried Pfeiffer (1899-1961, a scientist) was my godfather. Eugen Kolisko (1893-1939, a teacher and school doctor) often came to visit us on his way to London. Elisabeth Vreede (1879-1943, member of the Vorstand and leader of the Mathematics and Astronomy Section) spent a couple of days in Holland nearly every month, for the Vorstand had entrusted her with overseeing the Waldorf school in The Hague. My clearest memories are of Vreede—chiefly of her observing our lessons at school or sitting with us at the table with a rather wooden expression. I formed a strong bond with her after she died. I think that she had great spiritual integrity.

WW: What do you mean?

Emanuel Zeylmans: She had an uncompromising honesty towards herself and all other anthroposophists, and anthroposophy itself, to the point of self-effacement. That is the gesture of the consciousness soul. Through Vreede I had my deepest experience of the consciousness soul.

Ita Wegman (Ostern 1928)

**WW:** Did you also meet Wegman when you were a child?

**Emanuel Zeylmans:** Yes, but I have only one clear memory of her. I was probably about three. I climbed up to my father's study in my pajamas to say goodnight to him. I can still see myself standing there in this room, and opposite me was Ita Wegman. The study was decorated in a lovely dark blue, and Ita Wegman wore a black dress. She looked down at me and gave me a radiant smile, especially warm. That is a strong memory I have, which has remained with me ever since.

**WW:** She is said to have been there at your christening.

**Emanuel Zeylmans:** Yes, I found this out from one of my mother's diaries which I inherited at her death. She wrote some things in it about my christening. She also recorded a dream which she had shortly before I was born. She dreamed I was about to be born, but instead of me came first a small Mary figure, then Joseph, then the Christ child, and finally the shepherds and kings. She wrote:

All of them were made of a fluid substance that became hard as the figures were born. Then they looked like transparent, white wax. The Mary figure was particularly mysterious, with her folded hands. Wim [my father] took each one carefully in his hands and arranged them. And Aunt Sanne [Frau Bruinier] was also there. When all these little beings had been born, Emanuel finally emerged. I no longer clearly remember how he looked.

This was my mother's description of her dream; but the dream continued:

After the birth I went into the White Room, where a group of people were doing eurythmy. Pfeiffer was sitting there at the piano.

I find this dream of my mother's shortly before my birth remarkable because the Christian Community started in the Goetheanum's White Room; and in 1964, after my mother had died, I became a priest in this Christian Community. My mother knew the White Room because she had completed her eurythmy training there.

### And it was there that the little fellow saw Ita Wegman for the first time

Two other children of anthroposophical parents were christened at the same time as me. This was in October 1926 in The Hague. The Christian Community had just been founded there. In those days people thought a child should have four godparents, so there were twelve godparents gathered there for the three christenings! That seems ridiculous to us nowadays, but it was one of the peculiarities of those pioneering times. At the same time as the christening there was an international conference on Waldorf education in The Hague, so that it was easy to choose these godparents from the participants. My mother wrote in her diary,

"And it was there that the little fellow saw Ita Wegman for the first time. Grete Bockholt carried him on her arm. I didn't witness it myself, but it must have been wonderful to see how he gazed at Frau Dr. Wegman without interruption. Veronika [my older sister] said that Dr. Steiner knows Emanuel, because he is in heaven, and that's where Emanuel has just come from."

**WW:** Did Ita Wegman also come to observe your class at school?

**Emanuel Zeylmans:** Yes, my class-teacher told me this. When she told me, I could faintly recall vague images of it. I had a telephone conversation with my old class-teacher shortly before her death, in which I asked her whether she had known Ita Wegman. She replied: "She was with you in the classroom. She always sat at the back." I don't know why she was there, she may have been advising the school doctor.

### Goethe's fairytale: a golden treasure of a memory

**WW:** One of your deepest childhood experiences was when your teachers performed Goethe's fairytale. What impressions do you retain of this?

**Emanuel Zeylmans:** That is one of my most beautiful memories. My teachers performed this fairy-tale by Goethe in 1931 or 1932. Some of the teachers at the Waldorf school in The Hague formed a theatre group with the Munich actor Max Gümbel-Seiling, who came to live in Holland after the Stakenberg camp. Our teachers gave the most beautiful performances of the whole story, of all its mysterious, colorful scenes. I held my breath as I saw the kings in their underground temple, when the old one strikes the green snake with the lamp. Quiet as mice in the crowded hall we listened to the wonderful promises of a bridge that would one day be built over the river. The two will-o-the-wisps were terribly funny, and were played by the longest, thinnest teachers. The giant was also unforgettable: he had tied blocks of wood to his feet and stamped about recklessly through the play, larger than life. As the actors made their way over the bridge with the dead prince at the midnight hour, they sang a strangely affecting song—in fact the whole play was full of music. The whole thing remains in my memory as a living, golden treasure.

**WW:** Did the fairytale also have special significance for Ita Wegman?

**Emanuel Zeylmans:** Yes. I found out that she did not have any particular interest in Rudolf Steiner during the period after she first met him. Although they both lived for awhile in Berlin at the same time as each other, she was more interested in social concerns, methods of healing, massage, and all sorts of reform movements. The theosophists, in contrast, were involved in quite different things between 1902-1904, with no particular understanding of social problems. But it was because of such social questions that Ita Wegman first came to Berlin. She only visited him to make his acquaintance. I described the esoteric background to this fairytale, based on Steiner's descriptions from 1924, in an essay published in 1995.

From Steiner's 1924 account, one can conclude that, before her birth, Ita Wegman's soul drew from the spiritual source of this fairytale, from the place whence it arose.

## *The college of teachers split down the middle*

**WW:** While you were at the Waldorf school in The Hague, the conflicts in the Anthroposophical Society were raging in Dornach; and soon after this came the Second World War. How did you experience this time? How was the college of teachers affected by these problems?

**Emanuel Zeylmans:** I don't have any memories of the conflicts in the Anthroposophical Society that relate to my parents— as a child I was unaware of this. My sister, who is four years older than me, and with whom I later spoke about these things, could remember one or two things. For instance she remembered my father shaving and talking to himself in the mirror in an agitated

Ita Wegman in Berlin (1899)

kind of way. My older sister had a profound sense of how unhappy
and miserable my father felt because of these Society conflicts.
Although he was good at standing up for himself, these problems
affected him very deeply, for he felt that a part of Steiner's life's
work was being destroyed.

Nor did I pick up on these conflicts at school. I probably wasn't
the type to be interested in such things. But when I was fifteen,
the German Nazis outlawed the Dutch Waldorf schools, and that
affected me profoundly. I found it tragic, appalling. Later I went
to see my former class-teacher and he told me that the Nazis' clo-
sure of the schools had been a great relief for the college of teachers of the Hague school, because they were finally freed from
having to work together.

**W W:** Really?

**Emanuel Zeylmans:** Yes. That's how difficult things were
between the Waldorf teachers! They had been finding it very difficult to work together for eighteen years, but I had little direct
sense of this as a pupil. I know there were various groupings

among the teachers, and a few fanatics—even two teachers who became Nazis. One shouldn't forget that there were also a considerable number of Nazis in Holland.

While I was working on the Ita Wegman biography it dawned on me that I had been somehow aware of this split in the college and the conflicts in the Society which caused them, but without knowing the reason. For instance I saw how teachers behaved to one another, how odd this way of relating to each other was. I can also remember a female teacher bursting into tears. But all that I was aware of was this lack of emotional harmony.

**WW:** Did the Nazis clear everyone out of the school?

**Emanuel Zeylmans:** When Waldorf schools were prohibited and the buildings seized, we were moved out and had to go, as a whole school community, to another school. A secondary school offered to take all the pupils from the Waldorf school.

### Arrested as a spy

**WW:** Did you complete your Abitur (leaving exams) there?

**Emanuel Zeylmans:** No, I never took my Abitur. I only stayed a year and a half at this secondary school and then I continued my studies in the Royal Library. I found that much more interesting—I had access to any books I wanted. As a sixteen- and seventeen-year-old I studied, for instance, the Greeks' battle for liberation against the Turks, translated Baudelaire, and much more. It was roughly at this time that I left home; and in the summer of 1944, while illegally crossing the border to Germany, the border police arrested me. I had to spend six weeks on remand in a German women's prison. They arrested me on suspicion of spying. There were mainly French women in this prison who had hidden English pilots. I was in solitary confinement. While I was there I often sang songs to entertain the prison inmates.

**WW:** It doesn't sound as though this prison experience was too dreadful for you!

**Emanuel Zeylmans:** I grew very thin, but otherwise it was a rather fine experience, for I came to myself once more. A week after my arrest my father received a letter from the Geilenkirchen prison director, saying that I had been arrested on suspicion of spying while illegally crossing the border. He went straight to the chief of police in The Hague—a great resistance fighter against the Nazis, who later lost his life as a result—and urged him to write a letter saying that Dr. Zeylmans was someone who had an excellent relationship with Germany. That was true in fact, although he had no contact with Nazi circles. Because of this intervention I was released after six weeks.

## The Grandmother

**WW:** You had a special relationship with your grandmother on your mother's side. What sort of woman was she?

**Emanuel Zeylmans:** She was a choleric, very energetic, almost fanatical women's rights activist. She was interested in all social and political issues. As an anthroposophist she was always preoccupied with politics and history. She had an extremely unconventional view of life and brought up her three daughters—my mother being the eldest—in a fairly unconventional way. Together with a few other parents she founded a new school for her two older daughters. Then she was active in helping to found the Waldorf school in The Hague in 1922/23, so that her third daughter, who still lives in Switzerland, could go there. On meeting Rudolf Steiner she saw that he was, for her, the greatest contemporary figure. She could tell such fascinating stories that my mother sometimes had to tell her to stop because otherwise I wouldn't have fallen asleep.

She was married to Rotterdam's Lord Mayor. My grandfather was at the same time a member of parliament, member of the League of Nations, and chairman of the international trade association. But my grandmother did not live with him in the socially accepted sense—they separated but remained the best of friends. She moved to The Hague, he remained in Rotterdam. My grandfather was also a freemason. All this had a decisive influence on me as a child.

My grandmother suffered a good deal from the difficulties in the Anthroposophical Society, in fact they represented a rupture in her own life. She was close to going to pieces from the strictures this placed on her, her own impotence, for she had thrown everything into anthroposophy, e.g., had organized conferences and congresses. It was she who brought Rudolf Steiner to Holland in 1922.

I have the deepest connection with my grandmother. When I go to a concert nowadays she always sits beside me.

**WW:** Why concerts particularly?

**Emanuel Zeylmans:** Perhaps because she is very closely connected with Inspiration, with hearing. She sits next to me with her choleric soul and her burning power of devotion, which still unites her with the earth. I knew another such choleric: Dora Krück von Poturzyn (1896-1968, writer). I dedicated the first volume of my Ita Wegman biography to her. She was always looking over my shoulder while I was writing, from the world beyond, to see if I was doing everything right.

### Aunt Sanne

**WW:** Was anyone else in your family connected with anthroposophy?

**Emanuel Zeylmans:** Yes, Aunt Sanne was. There is a photograph of her in the biography of my father—she is standing next to my mother. Sanne is a short form for the French name Jeanne. She was called Jeanne Bruinier. Aunt Sanne painted the "I-child" in the First Goetheanum. It's a detail in the cupola paintings there. I have a sketch for it here, on which you can still see burnmarks from the fire that burned down the First Goetheanum. Steiner commissioned her to paint this "I-child." In her letters to her sister—my grandmother—she describes how difficult this was. Before the First World War she lived as a painter in Warsaw, then from 1914-1922 in Dornach. After the Goetheanum fire she moved to Holland and stopped painting. She began to give speech formation lessons.

Jeanne Bruiner's sketch for "I-child"

It was my fate to learn French as a young boy with my great aunt Sanne. In all I had language lessons with her every week for over twelve years. When I was secondary school age she also taught me English. During these lessons she would only speak French or English. Strangely enough I could speak fluent French and English with her then, but later these two languages became very alien to me. I had a strong experience of her lessons—not as particularly pleasant, but very vivid. She was a genius as a language teacher and had also helped many teachers at the Waldorf school in The Hague. She had also translated the Oberufer Christmas plays into an old Dutch dialect—she had witnessed Steiner directing these plays in Dornach. When I was directing them myself later with a group of young people, I went to her and she passed on to me the smallest details of the Dornach performances.

**W W**: Was your great aunt a member of the esoteric school?

**Emanuel Zeylmans**: Yes. After her death my father—as though this was perfectly natural—passed on to me her esoteric notes. These were mantras, the "accompanying exercises" and other notes. Since then I have had a quite different connection with this great aunt, for I have tried to practice the meditations she practiced. I am also particularly grateful that I learned precision of language in her French lessons, for I needed this when writing the Wegman biography. One can also formulate and depict things very precisely in German—which does not come easily to me as a Dutchman. My wife Cordula, and later Friedmut Körner, continually asked me whether I had written precisely what I meant. My great aunt was, as it were, the godparent to this process of self-education.

### I began to be interested in esoteric matters

**W W**: Did you have a relationship to esoteric matters when you were young?

**Emanuel Zeylmans**: Certainly not consciously. But in the last years of the war I made contact in Amsterdam with a circle of Stefan George followers, led by Wolfgang Frommel. Wolfgang Frommel sometimes showed that he knew a great deal about esoteric and occult movements, and this woke me up to occultism. My great aunt, in contrast, never referred to anything esoteric during her life. I would never have known that she was a member of the esoteric school.

Then a very peculiar period of destiny began for me. In 1953 I married my first wife, a Jewish writer, who is a professor emeritus in Amsterdam. She wanted me to tell her all about anthroposophy. Although I was not in the least interested, she asked me very penetrating questions. By having to tell her all about the Christmas Foundation Meeting, world evolution, reincarnation and karma, fourfold human being, etc. I raised all these things, which before had been slumbering unconsciously in me, into my own consciousness.

We had difficult crises in our marriage and at some point I began to dream about Rudolf Steiner. So outwardly, descriptions of anthroposophy were drawn from my mouth, as it were, while inwardly, in my soul, images or memories of Rudolf Steiner surfaced. These related to the way his language is so different at different times—the spoken word, his philosophical writings, his esoteric descriptions—such as in *An Outline of Esoteric Science*—and his verses and meditations. I have to regard this time of my life as a threshold experience, in other words a moment of destiny that can only be assessed in esoteric terms.

## *A wonderful cultural world began to blossom*

**WW:** For a Dutchman you have always had a strong connection with Germany. What relationship do you have to both nations and languages?

**Emanuel Zeylmans:** I have a more soulful connection with my own nation, probably because I was born there and lived there for forty years. I came to know German culture through the Georg followers in Amsterdam, a circle of literary people who had gone underground to flee the Nazis. In 1951, I founded with them the German magazine *Castrum Peregrini*. That in itself is a strange destiny, that I as Dutchman in anti-German Holland helped found a German-language magazine!

**Cordula Zeylmans:** One has the impression that these Georg circles stood guard over Germany's spiritual inheritance, while in Germany itself in the Nazi period...

**Emanuel Zeylmans:** ...it was being desecrated. In anthroposophical circles too, this spirituality was nurtured, though in a different way.

**WW:** Can you give more of a description of this Georg circle?

**Emanuel Zeylmans:** We cultivated the German language through regular readings. There were proper poetry readings, even as the Gestapo raged outside on the streets. I found this circle of people in 1944, immediately on my release from prison. I also met Percy Gothein there, who belonged to the Staufenberg circle.

**WW:** How did you make contact with these people?

**Emanuel Zeylmans:** The friend with whom I opened the small bookshop in Amsterdam was as interested in literature as I was. One day a foreign man spoke to him in a bookshop. It was Wolfgang Frommel from the Georg circle. My friend called me to Amsterdam and introduced us. The group had an atmosphere of some secrecy, for all the members were immigrants. Most of them lived together in the same house in Amsterdam. There were also some very strange figures who went there, such as the painter Max Beckmann. Many Jews lived there, a few Poles, and Czechs. The house was crammed full of refugees—and they all survived.

**WW:** Where was this?

**Emanuel Zeylmans:** It was at 401 Heeregracht. The house itself was in the shape of a ship's prow. It was very difficult to get inside. When you rang nothing happened. But as you were ringing you were being watched through a mirror. The woman who later married the mayor of Amsterdam had taken these people under her protection and rented them the upper floors.

That was a very romantic, but at the same time dramatic, life-threatening situation. None of these people left the building for three years. They survived by writing poetry, translating, and studying different subjects. Some of them later became professors. They kept going by taking up the German language and German humanistic culture as their inmost ideal.

**WW:** And you founded the magazine *Castrum Peregrini* under the influence of this group?

**Emanuel Zeylmans:** During the war these people had found that poetry and active involvement with literature is a profound source of life and strength. Jacques Lusseyran (1924–1971, professor of French literature) found the same thing in the concentration camp, when he helped people to find new courage by reciting French poems. The Georg circle experienced this more intensely and over a longer period. As it was with the monks of the Middle Ages, a wonderful cultural world began to blossom for them.

Then came the liberation from the German occupation, and soon a flood of visitors poured in. It turned out that there were many international links here between people, so a sort of cultural center arose. Wolfgang Frommel was the focus of this—he was the son of a professor from Heidelberg, and was a very cultivated, humorous, sociable man.

## *Castrum Peregrini*

He was the friend of a wealthy Swiss woman, who visited him in Amsterdam. One day she invited Wolfgang Frommel and myself to a restaurant, and during the meal launched the idea of starting a magazine. That was at the end of 1949. At the time I did not know what profession to choose, so I was open for such a plan. Frommel was aware of this of course. We called the magazine *Castrum Peregrini*, which was the code name for the house in which the immigrants had hidden, and means "pilgrims' castle of refuge," a term that came from the old Templar castles.

To be brief, I was very keen and we received the funding to start the operation. A friend was also very enthusiastic about the *Castrum Peregrini* magazine. So for the first one and a half years I also had some kind of basic income.

In the cellar of the old cottage where I lived at the time, there stood thousands of unused card-index files belonging to a former textile firm. I went to Wolfgang Frommel with these and got out of him 2,500 addresses of the people he knew all over the world. That's what kind of man he was—do you know anyone who could come up with 2,500 addresses of friends and acquaintances from their old address books? It took

Emanuel Zeylmans (1950)

me several weeks to transfer all these to the card-indexes. I sent all of them a wonderful brochure, which was financed by the Swiss lady, and—you'll hardly believe it—600 of these people took out a subscription to *Castrum Peregrini*.

**W W:** How long did you stay involved with this magazine?

**Emanuel Zeylmans:** Until 1954. *Castrum Peregrini* is still going today. It consists mainly of literary contributions and research. The magazine is now forty-five years old and has won several prizes. It has become a very well-regarded specialist magazine, still based in Amsterdam.

Working on this magazine, however, did not give me enough of an income, for by then I had a wife and child. The typesetter of *Castrum Peregrini* noticed that I was close to starving, and got me a job at the Post Office in The Hague. I became editor of an inhouse magazine. Every month for five years I wrote the copy for the entire magazine. That's how I learned to write.

**W W:** Didn't you write articles for *Castrum Peregrini*?

**Emanuel Zeylmans:** No, I was only the editor and managed the administration and correspondence. My first wife was a very gifted writer, could think very clearly and express herself well, so she helped me with the Post Office magazine. In the first year she corrected all of my articles.

## The most difficult years of my life

**W W:** Later on you worked for five years for the publisher Pieter de Haan (1891-1968). What did you learn there that helped you with your work on the Ita Wegman biography?

**Emanuel Zeylmans:** I trained and gained a qualification in publishing. Pieter de Haan himself had been a theosophist since 1912, had encountered Rudolf Steiner in many different situations, and was also a member of the esoteric school. He was a very warm-hearted man and a friend of my father. When I entered Pieter de Haan's publishing company I had five years as a state employee behind me, and now I found myself in this little firm which was run like a trading company. Pieter de Haan was a very

Pieter de Haan

emotional person. He had a heart of gold but could also rage at you like a madman.

I didn't cope very well with that. I spent the five most difficult years of my life there.

**WW:** You mean because of the difficulties with Pieter de Haan?

**Emanuel Zeylmans:** Yes. He was in a very odd position. He had retired shortly before I joined the firm, wishing to have a calmer, more reflective life. His much younger colleague took over the publishing company, but suddenly died of a heart attack. So de Haan had to come back. He was sixty-six and all his hopes of living a life free of publishing work were gone at one fell swoop. The company had thirty employees. I had said to him that he should think of me if he ever wanted a good manager's secretary. Just one day later he offered me this position. I agreed and found myself in a situation which was far too much for me to handle.

After five bitter years as a publisher I realized that I should have first learned to be a businessman. A publishing company needs a good businessman to survive. But just as important is a wide education and culture, and a sense for good books so that the company has a proper program. This combination of being cultured and having real talent as a businessman is the mark of a good publisher. In these five years I came to see that neither the one nor the other really lived in me as compelling interests. But Pieter de Haan kept hoping that I could become his successor.

**WW:** Was it an anthroposophical publishing company?

**Emanuel Zeylmans:** No, although it also published anthroposophical books. There was no market for them in Holland at the time, and they only appeared in very small editions.

## *I was searching for Christ*

**WW:** In 1964 you went to the Christian Community's Priest Seminar in Stuttgart. What led you to this?

**Emanuel Zeylmans:** In 1963, I came to the conclusion that I was not suited to the publishing profession. My wife and I also divorced the same year. So it was a difficult time for me, both professionally and personally. I asked myself at the time what I really wanted to do here on earth and I got the sense that I was on the wrong side of the river. What I was really seeking was over there on the other side.

I felt I had gone more and more astray as a publisher. In the meantime I had become assistant director and was co-signatory on all our contracts. We were just planning a series of about 100 scientific books, which were also to be translated into nine languages. At this time I had the feeling that among these hundred authors there would certainly be some actively opposed to anthroposophy. I had the image in my head of a beautiful forest region of Finland that would have to be felled to provide the paper for these books. Of course these were only passing reflections, but by now I was thirty-six and thinking hard about what I should do with my life. I wanted to start something that wasn't egocentric, and that could make a positive contribution to life. I also wanted to find a profession that offered sustenance in a Christian sense.

At about this time I first developed a relationship to religious rites. On the evening of Good Friday 1963 I attended the Easter service at a little Russian Orthodox church in Rotterdam. When I tried to take communion there, I was told that I first had to be baptized in the Russian Orthodox Church. So at the crack of dawn on Easter Sunday I drove to Zeist and arrived just in time to take part in the Christian Community's Easter service, and take communion. For me that was a natural step, for I was seeking Christ.

In this time of crisis I had many intense experiences; and one day—I remember this very well—it was suddenly clear to me that in reality I had only two choices: either to be a priest or a doctor. Now studying to be a doctor simply wasn't possible. I was poor and at the age of thirty-six could never have coped intellectually with such study! So the only alternative was to become a priest. But how?

In the very same hour this dawned on me, I wrote to Gottfried Husemann (1900-1972, priest and Oberlenker [similar to bishop] of the Christian Community, and director of the Priest Seminar). A few days later I was invited to discuss things with him. I was offered a place at the Priest Seminar and then I handed in my notice at the firm. Soon after I left, Pieter de Haan left also. The publishing house fell into financial difficulties soon afterwards and was bought up by another publisher. If I had stayed I would have fallen on hard times.

**W W:** How did your family and your anthroposophical friends react to the news that you were going to become a Christian Community priest?

**Emanuel Zeylmans:** My father-in-law, an older, non-anthroposophical doctor, was indignant and told me angrily: "You could have been the director of a publishing company, and instead you're choosing a life of poverty!" My younger brother was completely baffled, he simply couldn't understand it. My parents were no longer alive by then. When my older friend, Dora Krück von Porturzyn, with whom I had a lot of contact (I had also published translations of her books) heard of my decision, she told her friend: "Now we've lost a fellow fighter for the anthroposophical cause!"

Dora Krück von Poturzyn

Later on, when I was about to be ordained, I and some student friends and priests visited Margareta Morgenstern (1878-1968), Christian Morgenstern's widow. She asked more or less the same question as you have done: "Herr Zeylmans, what would your father say of your decision?" I replied: "Well, he would have been very surprised to say the least," to which she responded: "Aha, Herr Zeylmans, I see you are a diplomat like your father!"

## *A blessing and grace*

**WW:** What inner changes did you undergo in training to be a priest?

**Emanuel Zeylmans:** It was an inner healing. In retrospect I am unendingly grateful for this time of study. I was most profoundly affected by Rudolf Frieling (1901-1986, priest and third Erzoberlenker [similar to archbishop] of the Christian Community. Encountering Friedrich Benesch (1907-1991, priest of the Christian Community, director of the Priest Seminar after Husemann) and also Dieter Lauenstein (1914-1990, Christian Community priest) was also decisively important for me. My studies at the Priest Seminar were for me a constantly illuminating and clarifying process, and it was a blessing and grace for my life that I could become a priest.

**WW:** Once you had been ordained you returned to Holland. Was this a difficult time for you?

**Emanuel Zeylmans:** Yes, it is difficult to work in circles where you are known best as your father's son rather than as a separate, independent adult. My father guided anthroposophical undertakings in Holland for almost forty years. As his son I found it hard to breathe freely in such circles. Besides this, it also increasingly pained me to celebrate the Act of Consecration of Man in Dutch. It really made me ill. I felt at home in the original German of Steiner's texts and verses and in the words of the sacrament. The Dutch always felt like a translation to me. As well as this I had overtaxed myself in founding the magazine *Jonas*. I returned to Germany because I realized that the German language is healing for me. I needed its strength and form.

**WW:** You met your second wife at the Priest Seminar. She gradually became your closest collaborator. How was your first encounter with her?

**Emanuel Zeylmans:** She was also studying at the Priest Seminar. While I was training, Friedrich Benesch once asked whether one of us students could play the role of Saint Nicholas for a few families and children. I said I would and had to organize it—including finding a Knecht Ruprecht. I asked Cordula Schmidt if she would be willing to be my Ruprecht. I had already noticed her before in a course given by Benesch on Steiner's philosophical ideas because she had asked a question about the consciousness soul. She had asked whether it wasn't characteristic of the consciousness soul to refrain from answering a question posed to a group of students, if one knew the answer, so as not to bring the process of seeking an answer to a premature end. Thirty-two years later I still have a clear memory of her asking this. I had already been separated for more than three years, and it was very important to me to find a partner. It was then that I suddenly saw what lived in her.

**Cordula Zeylmans:** Out of this situation, I decided to renounce the profession of priest myself. From the beginning this was accompanied by what seemed to me an intense questioning from the other world, from his parents, whom I had sensed as very close to me, familiar, only a short time before, when I read Willem Zeylmans' book *Gespräche über die Hygiene der Seele* (Conversations on the health of the soul, Arlesheim 1988). So despite the weightiness of this decision, I had no doubts about it.

**Emanuel Zeylmans:** My wife was someone who, for the first time in years, I experienced as being on the same path as myself. It wasn't ardent love to begin with, but the fact that we were on this same path that brought us together. And I am very grateful for the fact that she said "yes" at the time.

## My first book

**W W:** How did you come to write a biography of your father? When did you write it and how long did it take?

**Emanuel Zeylmans:** I had inherited his literary estate and had to organize all his writings: in the process I came across a huge number of anthroposophical articles and poems. I gradually worked my way through this wealth of writings over the years. I had been working as a Christian Community priest in Holland for about six years when I fell ill and had to convalesce. I moved my family to southern Germany so that I could work as a gardener. It was at this time that I received a request from a Dutch publisher to translate my father's book, *The Foundation Stone*, into Dutch. My father had written all his books in Dutch except this one, which he wrote in German, in collaboration with Krück von Poturzyn. He wrote it in German because it deals with Rudolf Steiner's Foundation Stone verses. The book explains and clarifies the Christmas Foundation Meeting meditation. Up until 1974, no one dared translate the Foundation Stone meditation into Dutch.

**W W:** Why not?

**Emanuel Zeylmans:** Most Dutch people knew German. Perhaps the being of anthroposophy had not yet sufficiently incarnated into the Dutch language. This was different in the Christian Community, for all the ritual texts had been translated into Dutch. My aunt Sanne, by the way, helped translate these. I celebrated the rituals in words she had translated.

Anyway, I agreed to translate my father's book into Dutch, for I had been fated to live intensely in both the German and Dutch languages. So while life itself led me from Holland back to Germany, I translated my father's book from German into Dutch.

**W W:** Was it difficult to translate?

**Emanuel Zeylmans:** Yes, I struggled a great deal, for many words of the Foundation Stone verses do not have any equivalent in Dutch, or have a different meaning. In the end I came up with a kind of draft version in Dutch and printed this in the newsletter of the Dutch Anthroposophical Society, at the same time asking for help with its translation. Thirty Dutch anthroposophists felt moved to respond and help me. For months I corresponded with these thirty people so as to arrive at the best possible translation of the Foundation Stone meditation. In the meanwhile I finished translating the rest of the book so that it could appear soon afterwards.

While doing this translation I discovered the guiding thread in my father's spiritual life—the Foundation Stone theme itself.

**W W:** Has your translation of the Foundation Stone verses been altered at all since then?

**Emanuel Zeylmans:** Yes, a little, unfortunately. Later I also translated into Dutch, *Laying the Foundation Stone of the General Anthroposophical Society*, which is an extract from GA 260. This contains the Foundation Stone meditation and Steiner's accompanying words at the Christmas Foundation Meeting.

**W W:** Did your discovery of the guiding spiritual thread in your father's life give you the impetus to write his biography?

**Emanuel Zeylmans:** In 1978, I heard of plans to compile a book in memory of my father. Actually I wasn't particularly in agreement with some of the people who wanted to write this. At the same time I visited an old publisher from Arlesheim, Dr. Andreas von Grunelius (1900-1987, director of the Natura publishing company), whose sister had been a doctor in the circle around Ita Wegman and Rudolf Steiner. Grunelius asked me to

Emanuel Zeylmans (1977)

write a book about my father in the place of this other book that several ladies were planning. I spent days telling him about my father's life, for instance that almost everything had gone wrong for him, that his life was a whole collection of impulses that had come to nought and was therefore unsuitable as a biography. But the old man became ever more enthusiastic and pointed out to me that the impulses are the most important thing in a person's life and that they show what someone is truly striving to attain. He directly urged me to write this book.

WW: How long did it take you?

**Emanuel Zeylmans:** It went surprisingly fast. My wife helped me a great deal. I finished it in three months. Working on this, my first book, was a wonderful time for me. During the beautiful summer days, I wrote page after page, two floors up in our house in Reutlingen. My wife was outside in the garden, and every few pages or so I asked her to read what I had written, dropping the pages down from the window. Then she sat there with a pen and made corrections. That's how the book came about, during the summer and autumn of 1979.

# III

# TWELVE YEARS' WORK ON
# THE WEGMAN DOCUMENTS

### The decisive meeting with Madeleine van Deventer

**WW:** On Ita Wegman's birthday (February 22) in 1980, you conceived the idea of writing her biography. On that day you wrote to Madeleine van Deventer. What did your letter say?

**Emanuel Zeylmans:** Among other things, I wrote:

> There is a matter on which I would like your advice, relating to a biography of Ita Wegman. I have been occupied with her for years. I have a single, very beautiful memory of her smiling at me...when I was a child. I have read everything she published, and the little memorial volume which others wrote about her, and now also the book with Dr. Steiner's verses. But despite this wealth of material, and the deeply affecting nature of the facts relating to her, it still seems to me that anthroposophists today cannot arrive at a real, living picture of her as an individual—except perhaps by putting arduous research into her life and getting a clearer picture of it through their own efforts.
>
> I am therefore wondering whether I could compile such a biography. I envisage a book that leaves all the "incarnation" questions to one side (there's the Kirchner-Bockholt book already, which speaks for itself). A book, therefore, which deals with her most recent life, written in a style easily accessible to a wider public, which would also enable readers to gain easier access to her writings.

I hope you are not shocked at this idea! I am also aware that there are enormous difficulties involved in this task, that make it well-nigh impossible—the collaboration with Dr. Steiner, the difficulties in the Society. But one surely ought to consider the many thousands of young people who will meet anthroposophy in the next few decades; and remember that the real nature of the Christmas Foundation Meeting needs to become ever more visible and accessible in future. We can also learn from Ita Wegman's life, through the biography of a contemporary human being, to develop and practice clearer perception of the secrets of karma. One ought to be able to get a sense of the incredible breadth and power of her previous incarnations through examining her present life. But we do not have the means at present.

I am not assuming that I am equal to this task. I would need several years of preparatory work before deciding. A biographer surely needs to develop a real relationship with his or her subject to get the sense that the person written about wants this, is involved, is there to help and inspire!

My question to you is: Do you think such a book would be suitable for Natura Verlag [publishers]? Could I rely on the collaboration of the administrators of Ita Wegman's literary estate? The book by Kirchner says (on page 11): "Ita Wegman left behind a surprising wealth of comments by Rudolf Steiner, both in prose and verse form, and in personal letters to her." Would I be allowed to see these? Would we be able to agree on a form of collaborative work?

**WW:** What was Madeleine van Deventer's position at the time?

**Emanuel Zeylmans:** She was Ita Wegman's successor as director of the Arlesheim clinic, though she had retired by 1980.

**WW:** She replied on the anniversary of Ita Wegman's death (March 4). What was her answer?

**Emanuel Zeylmans:** I can also quote verbatim from this letter:

Madeleine van Deventer

To be Ita Wegman's biographer is no easy task. But you know how to write and how to get to grips with a subject. The Society difficulties are no doubt a lesser part of the problem. The very finely differentiated relationship with Rudolf Steiner is more demanding.

I myself have written little about Ita Wegman, but spoken all the more. Until now the spoken word seemed to me the only possible means of being true to her being.

Between 1975 to 1977, I gave a number of lectures (celebrating her centenary), also in Stuttgart, among other places. Several thousand people heard these, and I believe that this corrected the picture people in the Society have of her. After the lecture I gave at the Goetheanum, Grosse (1906-1994, Vorstand member since 1956, chairman of the Society from 1966-1984): "You have returned Ita Wegman to us."

Without mention of "incarnations" of course!

It would be good if you could come to see me soon and spend several days. I will be glad to show you everything from Ita Wegman's literary estate. It includes about seven letters from Rudolf Steiner, which are not suitable for publication however.

There are no diaries, only drafts for lectures.

The verses and meditations will hardly be suitable either. These would have to be "surrounded" or carefully introduced, as I did with an Artemis verse [printed at the end of the Kirchner book].

There are about a hundred letters which Ita Wegman wrote to me, some of them "sunny" from her travels, but most of them "dark" with cares and worries [...]

The big question remains whether her individuality will allow anyone to write about her. Shortly before her death she told me: "The only thing I would like said at my cremation is that I will always serve Rudolf Steiner."

**WW:** Then you met Madeleine van Deventer. What can you tell us of these discussions?

**Emanuel Zeylmans:** I was well-prepared and had no end of questions. Since Madeleine van Deventer had retired by then, she didn't have much to do during the day, and I was able to spend three days with her. She told me about Ita Wegman for hours on end. During our discussions I saw how interested she was in me writing a biography of Ita Wegman, similar to the one I had written about my father.

For about three years after this I was able to come to see her repeatedly to ask her questions about Ita Wegman. At that time I still assumed I could write an easy, generally accessible book about her. I possessed a large, empty account book in which I drew up a first chronology of dates in Ita Wegman's life. Fra van Deventer, almost blind by then, peered at this book thinking I had already begun writing the biography. She had a wonderful sense of humor, had great trust in me and real hope that I would manage it. She had been the one, too, who had previously decided that Natura Verlag should ask me to write my father's biography. She reminded me a little of a church dignitary, and occasionally she would knock upon the table and announce her decisions to me in a dark-toned, masculine voice.

Already at our first conversation she gave me a folder containing 113 letters Ita Wegman had written to her. The correspondence stretched over about twenty years. As she handed them to me, she made it unmistakeably clear that no one else had ever seen them before, and that they were absolutely confidential. "But I am assuming that you are a discrete man—after all, you're a priest."

### *Two suitcases full of notebooks*

A few months later I visited her again, for I still had innumerable questions. But I had hardly arrived and begun to formulate my first one before she interrupted me to say: "Grunelius over in the wooden house has Dr. Wegman's handwritten notebooks. I've asked him to show them to you."

So I went over to Grunelius, entered his study and saw that he had spread out all these notebooks of Ita Wegman. They lay everywhere—on benches, tables, settees, chairs. There were about a hundred of them, and some were fairly thick books. The whole thing was chaos—none of the notebooks were dated. There were also two cardboard boxes full of manuscript pages.

Rather shocked by this chaos I went back to Frau van Deventer and told her that it simply wasn't possible for me to sit in Arlesheim for months sifting through notebooks and manuscripts, ordering them and evaluating them. At this she went silently to the telephone, called Grunelius and said: "Please pack everything up for Zeylmans, he's taking it with him now." That phrase "he's taking it with him now" was of

Andreas von Grunelius

course a great surprise to me, and I could only stammer an astonished farewell. This was in the late afternoon and I had just come back from holiday, so I had two suitcases with me full of holiday things and dirty laundry.

I swiftly unpacked my cases and squeezed all the notebooks and manuscripts into them, putting my dirty laundry into the cardboard boxes instead. Then I sent the boxes by post before setting off for Reutlingen the same evening.

**W W:** Didn't Grunelius object when you took all the notebooks with you?

**Emanuel Zeylmans:** He was subordinate to Deventer, so he had to do what she told him.

**W W:** What did the doctors at the clinic have to say about it?

**Emanuel Zeylmans:** They knew nothing of it at first. But the next day a doctor from the clinic's executive committee called me, to ask me what I had taken. When I told her that Frau van Deventer had given me permission, she was lost for words. Naturally she was very ill-at-ease for it was an astonishing state of affairs that almost all of Ita Wegman's documents had left the clinic for the first time.

### Ordering the chaos

**W W:** How did you get the notebooks into any kind of order?

**Emanuel Zeylmans:** It was a mammoth undertaking! I first had to read them all and pay a great deal of attention to every date that appeared anywhere in them. Of these 100 books, three or four at the most could be dated. The rest bore no dates. My wife suggested that I go away for awhile, for in order to make a careful chronology one needs a great deal of space, calm, and days and nights of very systematic concentration. I took a holiday, and in my holiday lodgings gradually made sense of the content of these notebooks, until I was able to date most of them and order them chronologically. Yet I had to acknowledge that I still did not know all the details of Ita Wegman's life. In fact it took years to draw up a complete chronology. There were also periods—

amounting to years—for which no notebooks existed. For some months on the other hand there were six or seven.

**WW:** What did these notebooks contain? Were they like diaries?

**Emanuel Zeylmans:** No, she never kept a diary, except in the crisis period of 1934. Firstly, they contained a large number of patient consultations, secondly, drafts for her articles and essays, and thirdly, drafts of her short addresses and words of greeting. They also contained drafts of letters to various people; and finally notes about books she had read. She was a very conscientious reader of Rudolf Steiner's lectures. All these notebooks—a few dozen more turned up over the years from other parts of the globe—contained texts which, at first glance, could not be dated: were they from 1920 or 1940? This was a wonderful first introduction to Ita Wegman's biography. Later I did the same with her many manuscripts—another two thousand pages or so. And finally, I spent years reading an estimated six thousand letters.

### Esoteric treasures in the safe

**WW:** Yet Frau van Deventer had not given you everything. Notes about esoteric matters were missing, and above all Rudolf Steiner's letters to Ita Wegman. Where were these kept and who eventually gave you access to these letters?

**Emanuel Zeylmans:** Frau van Deventer had made it clear from the beginning that there was no question of publishing the letters and esoteric notes. Yet she did let me read copies of Rudolf Steiner's letters to Ita Wegman. While I read them she stayed with me in the room. I wasn't even allowed to touch them.

Frau van Deventer died in January 1983. The esoteric notes were in a different archive altogether, in the safe of the Arlesheim clinic. No one got to see these, not even the doctors in those days. They were completely taboo. By the time Madeleine Deventer died I had made a good deal of progress with my researches. I minuted all the discussions I had with her so that her comments about Ita Wegman should not be lost, for she had a very precise power of recall. I noticed very few errors in her descriptions, although she was already very old, almost blind, and very hard of hearing. She also tried to strengthen me and motivate my will for writing this biography, and led me into the intimate world of others. For instance she described how Dr. Hans W. Zbinden (1899-1977, doctor, member and also chairman of the Rudolf Steiner Nachlassverwaltung [Administrators of Rudolf Steiner's estate]) read her Rudolf Steiner's Koberwitz letter to Ita Wegman. But this made my work continually more difficult, for I began to sense that the whole nature of my enterprise was changing. Writing a lively biography of my own father was quite different from exploring the life of one of Rudolf Steiner's most intimate pupils.

**WW:** Who took on Ita Wegman's literary estate after van Deventer's death?

**Emanuel Zeylmans:** Dr. Anton Gerretsen together with two other doctors. He is four years older than I and comes from Holland. We were at the Waldorf school in The Hague at the same time, and he is the son of a Christian Community priest. I developed a friendly connection with him in subsequent years. One day I told him quite openly that I could not get a single step further without seeing all the esoteric notes of the collaboration between Ita Wegman and Rudolf Steiner.

**WW:** When was that?

**Emanuel Zeylmans:** 1984. He then took me to the safe I referred to, in the clinic. Of course I was aware that I was being given very special treatment, for no one previously had been able to study all these notes and records properly. Only Erich Kirchner (1899-1975) had had a look at them, which had given rise to the book by him and Margarete Kirchner-Bockholt.

**WW:** How much material did you find in this safe?

**Emanuel Zeylmans:** About four large briefcases full. But these notes were of a completely different quality to the notebooks. Amongst them were slips of paper about the size of two stamps, which one could have puzzled over for half a lifetime. I was staying with Anton Gerrestsen at the time, and asked him to take two folders home with him, so that we could study them in peace. We pored over some of this material together for a whole afternoon.

I was able to learn an enormous amount from him, as I had done from van Deventer. We were able to have very open, frank discussions—something that comes from knowing each other from a young age. He has a scientific approach to anthroposophy, is familiar with esoteric matters and has always been very reticent about judging other people. I value him highly.

## A moment of destiny in my life

So we were sitting there talking. Suddenly he was called away by an emergency, at which he pressed the two folders containing esoteric material into my hands, and left me to study them. That's how much he trusted me already!

I hardly knew what I was doing and took the folders to my room. All night I studied Rudolf Steiner's letters, verses, mantras, and exercises. I am incapable of describing this experience. I was almost completely lifted out of myself. My state of soul can perhaps best be compared with that of someone who unexpectedly enters a beautiful church in which a service is being held— the stillness, the reverence of the many people gathered there, the great words of ritual which resound through the space, the light that is so different from elsewhere! This was the mood that filled me as I became aware during the night how Rudolf Steiner worked in an esoteric way with Ita Wegman between 1923 and 1925—hardly more than a year in all.

Then I replaced these papers in their folders and told myself: "This is a moment of destiny in your life. You have looked into a spiritual space of which you understand nothing, which really has nothing to do with you. This was a secret—that is esoteric—spiritual collaboration between two people who had already worked together for thousands of years in the Mystery temples of humanity.

**W W:** What happened after this night? Did you have to hand back the esoteric notes?

**Emanuel Zeylmans:** Of course. I also had to leave, for I had work to do. I had my parish in Reutlingen to look after. Of course

I was very short of sleep; but on the other hand I felt inwardly enlivened, as though I had spiritual wings.

**WW:** Did you ever get another chance to see these esoteric notes?

**Emanuel Zeylmans:** Yes. I developed such a good working relationship with Gerretsen that I was able to see anything I wanted. But I never made photocopies.

**WW:** Did you make written copies of the texts then?

**Emanuel Zeylmans:** Never without the knowledge of Anton Gerretsen. Once I copied something without Madeleine van Deventer knowing—but she noticed this straight away. It was a wonderful poem. Rudolf Steiner also wrote poems for Ita Wegman. At that time it was my greatest aim to write another book devoted to these esoteric notes alone.

**WW:** You mean that nothing that has not been published in the Kirchner-Bockholt book or in your biography has been published anywhere else, and is only to be found in the safe at Arlesheim?

**Emanuel Zeylmans:** That's right.

### A key to understanding former incarnations

**WW:** Among Rudolf Steiner's letters to Ita Wegman is the famous or notorious Koberwitz letter of June 11, 1924. What is special about this letter?

**Emanuel Zeylmans:** In my first volume of the Wegman biography I printed all of Steiner's letters to her without omitting or changing anything, for I wanted them preserved once and for all for history. The collaboration between Steiner and Wegman gave rise to verses which show the world that Rudolf Steiner saw in Wegman a person with whom he had worked closely in previous incarnations, in the context of the Mysteries. Those who study this carefully can also see that Steiner—though without naming either himself or Wegman—gave a whole series of lectures about this work of theirs. His audience, though, did not have the key to understanding that he was speaking of himself and Wegman.

# IV

# THE COLLABORATION BETWEEN
# ITA WEGMAN AND RUDOLF STEINER

## The Mysteries of Ephesus

**WW:** The heart of your Wegman biography is the seventh chapter of volume two. How were pupils prepared for initiation? What trials and probations did they have to endure?

**Emanuel Zeylmans:** Initiations always begin with trials. That, we are told, is how it was in ancient times and it is no doubt the same today. Of the Mystery school at Ephesus Rudolf Steiner tells us, though indirectly, that pupils had to learn to overcome their egotism in particular. He even speaks of the "eradication of egotism." The soul also had to learn to endure fear and anxiety.

**WW:** To what extent did pupils have to pass through the dreadful depths of the soul? To what extent were people made aware that the devil lives in each one of us?

**Emanuel Zeylmans:** I can only tell you what Steiner describes, and the accounts of some ancient authors. The soul must learn to become selfless. This was achieved by methods far more severe than we can imagine today. A modern person would not be able to bear it and would go mad or die.

**WW:** What were the stages of Imaginative consciousness at Ephesus?

**Emanuel Zeylmans:** Actual initiation took place in three stages or levels—first through the awakening of a kind of clairvoyance—in other words the soul was led to suprasensible visions. Then one passed through the stage of Inspiration—learning to live consciously in suprasensible sound experiences in which spiritual

Emanuel Zeylmans at Ephesus (1992)

light was also heard. Thirdly, one passed through the stage of Intuition.

At Ephesus the first stage of Imagination—Steiner calls it the "second Mystery chapter" because he sees the preparations and trials as the first "chapter"—are closely related to a schooling of the etheric body. Steiner once described how pupils were led before the great statue of Artemis, and had to devote themselves to it so profoundly, both by looking and touching, that they came to identify with the figure. The pupil who was to be initiated—both men and women were initiated at Ephesus, and teachers at the Mystery school were mainly women, called "bees"—identified with the goddess and then experienced nature with a transformed consciousness.

Statue of Artemis, marble, 1st century AD

**WW:** How could pupils learn to feel their way into the etheric world by means of the Artemis statue?

**Emanuel Zeylmans:** Through experiences of touch and vision.

**WW:** Were pupils also transported back to the far past during their visions?

**Emanuel Zeylmans:** Yes. Previous stages of the earth's evolution are of course present in the Akashic Records in the earth's memory. Through this, pupils experienced how everything was created.

**WW:** Was the pupil also led into the underworld?

**Emanuel Zeylmans:** That is how Steiner describes it. Modern depth psychology naturally links this with the unconscious depths of the soul. That is no doubt a valid point of view, although it isn't

Statue of Artemis, marble, 2nd century AD

the whole story. What is without is also within. But in Ephesus the focus was not on plumbing the depths of the human soul, but in disclosing the mysteries of the plant world—in other words the natural forces of the earth.

**WW:** At what time of day were the Imaginative exercises performed and experienced?

**Emanuel Zeylmans:** At night, by moonlight if possible.

**WW:** On December 27, 1923 (in GA 233) Steiner speaks about the element of Inspiration in the Ephesus Mysteries, the third stage or chapter in initiation. To what extent was language, the Word, used to initiate the novice into cosmic secrets?

**Emanuel Zeylmans:** The sounding of vowels and consonants was experienced through one's own speech. After all, the planets and the fixed stars—the celestial workings of the zodiac—work in to these elements of speech. Pupils had to practice exercises similar to speech formation, whereas for the previous second stage they had to learn to tend the earth in gardening.

**W W:** In Ephesus initiation, what did the exercises consist of at the level of Inspiration?

**Emanuel Zeylmans:** Learning to distinguish the workings of light in tones. This is also called discovering the harmony of the spheres.

**W W:** At what time of day was this practiced?

**Emanuel Zeylmans:** From Steiner's descriptions one can conclude that this was during the daytime.

**W W:** How did the pupil learn the secrets of the cosmic Logos?

**Emanuel Zeylmans:** Through purposeful, schooled speech.

**W W:** Is there a connection between the initiation site of Ephesus and the prologue to the Gospel of St. John?

**Emanuel Zeylmans:** Yes, the Gospel of St. John came about at Ephesus, in the first century AD. By then, though, the Mystery school had already been ineffective for many centuries. But its effects could certainly still be found in the etheric sphere. The Gospel of St. John begins, of course: "In the beginning was the Word, and the Word..." So everything had arisen through the Word. This expresses in a new way, through words, what ancient Mystery wisdom possessed as its deepest secret.

**W W:** So John was still inspired by Ephesus?

**Emanuel Zeylmans:** Yes, quite certainly. The whole Gospel of St. John is more connected to Inspiration than Imagination. It contains chapters with long passages of Christ's own words.

**W W:** What is the element of Intuition in the Ephesus Mysteries? Is it the conversation between pupil and teacher described by Steiner?

**Emanuel Zeylmans:** Yes, certainly, that's how Steiner describes it. One has to make something of an effort to understand this. For what occurs in a real, profound conversation? Verbal exchange enables the thoughts of the people conversing to move towards a common goal, their different experiences come together. A process of development begins, souls are given an impetus by one another and thus become productive.

The Temple of Artemis at Ephesus, by E. Falkner

One could also say that something is *born* that would not arise in a soul that is simply preoccupied with itself. Working together through conversation creates new insights.

**WW:** Initiation lasted three days?

**Emanuel Zeylmans:** I imagine so. Steiner did not state this directly in relation to Ephesus. But I assume that there were individual preparations for the various stages which lasted much longer.

**WW:** When did one enter the holy of holies, and what happened there?

**Emanuel Zeylmans:** The innermost sanctum was, according to Rudolf Steiner, the statue of the goddess. Not the "great statue" of later times, which stood outdoors on the western side of the temple, but the devotional image inside the temple. At Ephesus it was discovered that there had formerly been a large, unroofed interior on the eastern side. It may be that there was a small temple there, as in other Greek temples, and a flowing spring. The inner court was certainly full of plants.

**WW:** A particular characteristic of the Ephesus Mysteries was that initiation had to be performed by two people together—the initiate and the pupil. What did Enkidu and Gilgamesh experience in their reincarnation as initiates at Ephesus?

**Emanuel Zeylmans:** They experienced the loftiest secrets of all evolution, especially of the plant kingdom and the soul's preparations for birth.

**WW:** On the day that Alexander the Great was born (356 BC), Herostratus set fire to the Mystery site of Ephesus. Did Alexander the Great feel the urge to come to Asia so that he might return to Ephesus?

**Emanuel Zeylmans:** No, on the contrary, he felt this urge in order to spread the Mystery wisdom of Ephesus—which he had experienced in a previous incarnation—to the Far East.

### Redeeming elemental beings through new capacities of perception

**WW:** In the lecture cycle "Anthroposophy and the Human Soul," Rudolf Steiner speaks of the redemption of elemental beings through a particular way of seeing nature. What did Steiner mean by this?

**Emanuel Zeylmans:** He gave these lectures in Vienna at Michaelmas 1923. To her great surprise, Steiner called Wegman away from her work at the clinic and urged her to attend these lectures in Vienna. Reading the lecture of September 30, 1923 very carefully, one notices that it contains a passage of about one and a half pages whose connection with the context of the lecture is not quite clear. But a special light falls on this if one compares it with Steiner's descriptions, at Torquay in August 1924, of his collaboration with Wegman.

In the lecture of September 30, 1923 he describes in a few sentences the so-called Saturn path which he developed with Wegman for spiritual research into organs. If one also considers the description in the public lecture of September 27, 1923 (CW 84) then one comes upon one of anthroposophy's most central concerns in the last years of Rudolf Steiner's life. These lectures on anthroposophy and the human soul deal with the development of new powers of human perception. In particular they describe how the anthroposophist should try to practice a special way of looking at the plant kingdom. Very interestingly, he gives the example of the lily—which made me think of Goethe's fairytale of the green snake and the beautiful lily. Rudolf Steiner shows how elemental beings dwell in plants as in other realms of nature and that they can be redeemed through human perception, but only when we develop in our soul and our seeing a soul-spiritual relationship to a particular plant. Modern humans, having evolved a more and more material, object-focused perception, leave the elemental beings bound and fettered to the earth. But these elemental beings have a great longing to be included in human evolution, and only through us developing a new way of seeing can they be freed from their enchantment—from their imprisonment in matter.

A battle with the dragon is taking place at the scene of human consciousness. Nowadays our materialistic perception and thinking continually nourish the dragon forces within us. But by educating the soul to see in a new way, we starve the dragon instead.

## *Researching the underworld*

**WW:** How was the basis laid in the Ephesus Mysteries for the collaboration between teacher and pupil; and how did this ultimately lead to the initiate medicine that Steiner and Wegman created at the beginning of this century?

**Emanuel Zeylmans:** If one reads Rudolf Steiner's lectures on Ephesus, one gets some inkling of the way these two worked together in modern times. Even the way they collaborated 2,500 years ago at Ephesus—this intense collaboration of pupil and teacher—was, according to Steiner, an exception—a special thing. At that time the teacher could, through initiation, lift his perception into the world of forms—in anthroposophical terms the world of exusiae, the spirits of form. He ascended into these higher worlds and could there study the secrets of how formative forces work down into nature. The Mystery pupil—in this case the priestess, the incarnation of Ita Wegman's individuality—was sent down into the depths of the underworld through her Mystery schooling. There the pupil, unharmed like Persephone, could come to know the workings of the material world in nature.

Professor Karl Kerényi, and subsequently also Diether Lauenstein, have shown that this can be explained in terms of depth psychology, for we bear the underworld within us, in layers of our unconscious. But only Rudolf Steiner was able to fully solve this riddle, by showing how our nature connects us to the surrounding world. For the human being is also partly a natural creature. The significant thing is for us to expand our potential for consciousness to such an extent that the nature within us must no longer live in conflict with our true being. Then one also sees that the underworld is not only active in us, but is also a spiritual realm in nature. The underworld is also the world of demons. Wegman was able to research into it without coming to harm.

In 1934 Wegman fell severely ill, suffered from feverish conditions and foot inflammations and could hardly walk for months. At the time she had been making very intensive studies of the flora of the Swiss mountains and was able to use this outer, botanical knowledge in her medical practice. Ita Wegman describes this in the Persephone play she wrote for the Stakenberg youth camp in Holland, in the Easter weeks of 1930.

### The path of development of initiate medicine

**W W:** How did teacher and pupil work together in the field of initiate medicine so that the mystery or rather the cause of illness can be understood?

**Emanuel Zeylmans:** That is a very difficult question to answer, which many anthroposophical doctors have pondered over the years in their studies of GA 27, GA 243 and the lectures on medicine. In my view Rudolf Steiner describes a situation which does not generally apply to two researchers, but only to the initiate teacher and the Mystery pupil. Even the initiate, that is the Mystery teacher, cannot keep hold of certain things which are perceived clairvoyantly in the upper realm, in higher worlds. The very highest spiritual revelations are often swift, fleeting, and very hard to grasp. That is why the teacher needs a pupil with a connection to the underworld, who has corresponding experiences there. When both work together and, by conferring and conversing, recollect their experiences and researches and mutually augment them, then it is possible to grasp hold of the spiritual results of research, that is, to give them form in human speech. That is the method. Steiner said that this would one day become the science of the future.

In his last medical course which he gave to doctors and priests of the Christian Community, Steiner called this form of medical science "initiate medicine." He says there that the doctor should develop higher powers of knowledge than mere logic and reason. He is referring to powers of perception through which the doctor can investigate the patient's life body. Such powers can increase until the doctor can gradually perceive the astral body too, and ultimately can gain insight into the patient's destiny and the real origins of the illness. Steiner described this path of development in the first chapter of the book he wrote with Wegman. This first chapter is probably the last written text he ever composed. He wrote it long after the book had been completed, two or three days before his death.

**W W:** What was achieved through the collaboration between Steiner and Wegman? What would have been lacking in the world if they had not worked together in this way?

**Emanuel Zeylmans:** We would not have the outer institutes, such as the clinic at Arlesheim, but nor would we have practical karma research. Unfortunately I am not a doctor and so cannot speak of the medical aspects, which are really the important ones. Since Steiner's death the conviction has held sway in anthroposophical medical circles that the collaboration between Steiner and Wegman enabled something to enter the world, or try to, that would not otherwise have come about. One can sense that this is why Steiner worked so intensively with Ita Wegman in the last years of his life. Of course not everyone is interested in this, but if one holds this view one also has to ask the critical question as to whether the brief period of their collaboration created enough of a basis for this initiate medicine to take root and develop further. The question of whether this initiate medicine completely arrived on the earth or not is one that must remain open. I don't wish to comment on that.

WW: Steiner often waited for his pupils to ask questions before suggesting things or passing on new results of spiritual research. Ita Wegman asked the question about a renewal of Mystery medicine appropriate for our times. Did Steiner have to wait for this question before imparting spiritual-scientific aspects of medicine, or would he have been able to place aspects of this initiate medicine into the world without a pupil's question?

Emanuel Zeylmans: It is possible that Steiner also gave things which no one had asked for. That is hard to judge, of course, as he was also able to see what people were searching for or needed. But he indicated very clearly that his pupils should ask questions so that he could respond appropriately. That is connected with the fact that the initiate can only reveal what people on earth can render fruitful and make productive use of.

### *The meditative collaboration between Wegman and Steiner*

Cordula Zeylmans: Perhaps we shouldn't only look at the two figures of Steiner and Wegman, but also at the circle of people around them. Didn't these others also contribute to a renewal of Mystery medicine?

Emanuel Zeylmans: Of course the collaboration of a number of people is always necessary, and one ought actually to extend one's gaze still further. Among the many revolutionary comments by Rudolf Steiner is also the fact that in future people will not manage without the help of the dead. Even governments will, in the distant future, only be able to progress if they maintain a contact with the world of spirit. Otherwise everything on earth would disintegrate and go under. In the long-term the work of all people, of doctors too for instance, will no longer bear fruit if they do not practice collaboration with non-embodied spiritual beings. And Ita Wegman exercised this contact. In her meditations she always sought a connection with Rudolf Steiner's spirit, and acted from it. In 1924 Steiner prepared her intensively for this. She had, for instance, to practice a certain meditation with him each evening at eleven on the dot.

**WW:** Did the two meet together in person, or did they only meet in thought?

**Emanuel Zeylmans:** If they weren't at the same place Wegman had to turn her attention away from the conversations or activities she was engaged in and devote herself entirely to this meditation. There is a reference to this in the Koberwitz letters in the phrase: "I live in your meditation." From her notebooks I gathered that she sustained and practiced this contact with Rudolf Steiner as long as she lived. But her contemporaries did not perceive or acknowledge this. Rudolf Steiner had hoped that, in the esoteric Vorstand and in the esoteric doctors' circle, this spiritual activity would be treated with great seriousness and respect.

**WW:** Did Steiner carry out this meditation only with Wegman, or with other members of the Vorstand too?

**Emanuel Zeylmans:** I wasn't able to discover this because the Rudolf Steiner estate administrators pursue the principle that outsiders are not shown unpublished texts. I repeatedly asked them whether I could look at certain notebooks of whose existence I was aware, but they turned me down without more ado. So I cannot answer your question.

Steiner once remarked: "Members do not attend enough to the Christmas Foundation Meeting." I keep asking myself whether he was also referring to people in his close proximity? If one actively meditates for years with the rhythms of the Foundation Stone verses, one gradually finds an answer. In his closest proximity a profound and spiritual connection would have arisen—after his death too—if people had really cultivated these rhythms.

**WW:** When did the meditative work with Wegman begin?

**Emanuel Zeylmans:** That cannot be exactly dated, but certainly no later than September 2, 1923, in London. In the days before this both of them were in Wales, at Penmaenmawr, where she asked him about the new initiate medicine. Shortly after, in Vienna, while giving the lecture "Anthroposophy and the Human Soul," he decided to write the book *Fundamentals of Therapy* with her. From that time on one can follow their shared meditations.

**WW:** In this book Wegman writes: "Scientific medicine should not be underestimated in a superficial and dilettante way. This we fully acknowledged. But what was needed was to add to it what true spiritual knowledge can offer for understanding processes of illness and healing."

In GA 312 Steiner says, in contrast: "Today we can see how all the different schools [of medicine; WW] tend towards materialism. This is, in a certain sense, common to all of them. That is why the important thing is spiritualizing this whole realm."

Isn't spiritualization something quite different from simply adding spirit to what already exists?

**Emanuel Zeylmans:** I don't see such a contradiction there. It is true that Wegman and Steiner link up with materialistic science, start from there, but this materialism is only the natural scientific aspect, something that Steiner fully accepts. Above all he values the research methods and scientific basis of such work. What Steiner refers to in his lecture in 1920 as spiritualization of medicine is, in my view, what Ita Wegman describes a few years later in the book they wrote together. She says, for instance, that the real task is to introduce new ideas into medicine.

**WW:** Yet the question is whether one can extend all the fields and research of materialistic medicine through a spiritual approach, let alone spiritualize them. My question was to do with whether spiritualization might mean creating a wholly new initiate medicine out of the spirit, which in certain areas might be diametrically opposed to materialistic medicine.

**Emanuel Zeylmans:** This is a question, of course, which anthroposophical doctors debate. As far as I know, Rudolf Steiner has many different approaches to this. A new thinking, along the lines of the *Philosophy of Freedom (Intuitive Thinking as a Spiritual Path)*, would of course totally transform the philosophical bases of today's science, and also of medicine.

## *Wegman's decision at the Goetheanum fire*

**WW:** At the beginning of her collaboration with Rudolf Steiner, in 1923, Ita Wegman was not especially prominent within the Anthroposophical Society. But then the relationship between her and Steiner altered. A will component entered. What unleashed this activity?

**Emanuel Zeylmans:** From Ita Wegman's notes one can reconstruct when this happened. We see that up to the end of 1922 Rudolf Steiner always took the initiative in approaching Wegman's clinic, came to visit it, took part in patient consultations with increasing regularity, and engaged himself intensively on behalf of Wegman's work. On December 31, 1922 the first Goetheanum went up in flames, and we have the short but expressive description in Ita Wegman's handwriting to tell us that she saw the completely abandoned and lonely figure of Rudolf Steiner at the fire.

**WW:** That was her experience of the fire?

**Emanuel Zeylmans:** Yes. One suspects that the fire released in Wegman the first tentative memories of her former incarnations. The Goetheanum fire had an extraordinarily shocking and profound effect on many people, so certainly on Ita Wegman, too. She also had to give Rudolf Steiner medical attention, for he was in danger of collapse during that night. From that time on it is evident that she put herself wholly at his disposal. One can observe a very clear change of will during these days. She suddenly saw that she must put all her powers in the support of this man.

**WW:** What is the connection between the Goetheanum fire and the burning of the Ephesus Mystery site?

**Emanuel Zeylmans:** Rudolf Steiner described this. At Ephesus the secrets of the Logos, the secrets of world evolution, were studied and cultivated for centuries. According to Steiner the first Goetheanum was also a house of the Word. The whole conception of the first Goetheanum comes from the Logos Mysteries. Both temples were set on fire by opponents, and both were destroyed.

### The Mystery collaboration between Steiner and Wegman through six incarnations

**W W:** Why did Rudolf Steiner awaken consciousness of karma more strongly in Ita Wegman than in any other person, and why does he speak of her and his series of incarnations in a way different to any others, before members of the Anthroposophical Society?

**Emanuel Zeylmans:** The answer can only be that it lived powerfully in Rudof Steiner's awareness. For over a year he presented this series of incarnations to members of the Anthroposophical Society, and we simply have to accept this as a fact. The nine lectures of the 1923/24 Christmas Foundation Meeting are wholly devoted to this collaboration. In the karma lectures too, this theme keeps resurfacing. It was clearly a matter of the very deepest concern to him that his pupils and as wide as possible a circle of members should recognize this collaboration between him and Wegman. After all there had already been five preceding incarnations in which a very intensive collaboration existed between these two individuals. It begins in Chaldean–Babylonian times, at the time described in the Gilgamesh epic.

**W W:** To what extent is the background to Goethe's fairytale which Rudolf Steiner describes, connected with Ita Wegman's biography?

**Emanuel Zeylmans:** On July 18 and 19, 1924, Rudolf Steiner gave lectures to the anthroposophists in Arnheim. In these karma lectures he describes for the first time the great school of the Mysteries that the archangel Michael conducted in the world of spirit from the fifteenth to the seventeenth centuries. That was a kind of preparation for the earthly workings of anthroposophy in the twentieth century. Michael is the regent of Mystery schools. Steiner describes in Arnheim how the Mystery teachings for unincarnated human souls in the world of spirit culminated in a great ritual event at the end of the eighteenth and beginning of the nineteenth centuries. Steiner speaks of mighty imaginative pictures which appeared before these human souls during this spiritual event. Then follows his surprising comment that this cultic manifestation became noticeable for a few people on earth. Unfortunately he only gives one example. Goethe, he said, received Inspirations from this event in the spiritual world, and this led to his fairytale, *The Green Snake and the Beautiful Lily*.

It becomes clear from the karma lectures that the pair of whom we are speaking in this interview—Gilgamesh and Enkidu, who later incarnated as Alexander the Great and Aristotle—were very involved in initiating and sustaining this ritual event. The theme repeatedly surfaces that both souls worked together to carry and support this heavenly occurrence. He even once indicated that their collaboration enabled anthroposophy to be born—a significant statement of course.

It is therefore very apt that at the beginning of the twentieth century although Ita Wegman had known Steiner for awhile, and listened to his lectures, she did not approach him. But the moment Steiner spoke about Goethe's fairytale, he had her full attention and she was drawn to him. She was immediately accepted into his esoteric school.

# V

# MARIE STEINER AND EDITH MARYON

### *Rudolf Steiner's real mission*

**WW:** Steiner had already known the significance of his collaboration with Wegman for far longer. As early as 1910 he had spoken of some aspects of his and Wegman's series of incarnations, without mentioning any names. If it was one of his deepest concerns that the significance of this collaboration should be recognized by as many people as possible, how did it affect him when this same collaboration was doubted, mocked, and attacked by his closest colleagues and by many members?

**Emanuel Zeylmans:** Historically it is a very important thing that Walter Johannes Stein (1891-1957, history teacher) asked Steiner in 1922 what his most important mission was in his present life. Steiner replied that this was the teaching of reincarnation and karma. That, he said, was his real mission and everything else could have been done by others.

That Steiner was able to begin his comprehensive survey of karmic connections at the end of 1923 is related, in my view, to the fact that karmic perceptions dawned in Wegman's own soul. He therefore had a person before him for the first time whose soul experienced at least the beginnings of what he had been researching for decades. He could begin to speak of karma and reincarnation because at least one person was able to take it up fully into herself. Ita Wegman's visions soon intensified; gradually more and more memories of past lives arose in her, and so Steiner could begin with his true mission.

One simply has to take one's courage in both hands and imagine that all that Steiner did for his followers, or members of the

Anthroposophical Society, between 1902 and 1923, was a kind of
healing corrective, remedial work. In particular he corrected the
old theosophical teachings. In the collected works we find a flood
of corrections to these old views. He undertakes his corrections
out of a spirit that draws on the new Michaelic possibilities for
perception and knowledge described in *The Philosophy of Freedom
(Intuitive Thinking as a Spiritual Path)*. There he established these
new possibilities once and for all, and described them in a way
which others could follow. From 1902 onwards Rudolf Steiner
tried to think in harmony with human beings in this sense, so as
to liberate them from their thoroughly ailing, afflicted ideas of
civilization. But when he began his shared path with Ita Wegman in 1923, he again took up what he had left to one side at the
beginning of the century.

I became particularly aware of this through the work of Karen
Swassjan (professor of philology and philosophy), whose his philosophical studies describe what I have just referred to. Steiner's
language also becomes quite different in his "Anthroposophical Leading Thoughts" of 1924/25, and in the book he wrote
together with Wegman. This is also a help in better understanding Marie Steiner's karma in the Anthroposophical Society.

**WW:** How do you mean?

**Emanuel Zeylmans:** Marie Steiner belongs to this old theosophical world. She entered theosophical circles through Edouard
Schuré (1841–1929, French poet). Rudolf Steiner was also led into
these circles to undertake an esoteric task, to take care of these
people. That was, he said, the only useful thing he could do there.
This task, however, did not accord with Rudolf Steiner's own
will. Yet he took up this task among the theosophists with heart
and soul. This was possible for him because Marie Steiner, his
future wife, was fully accepted in these circles. Without her he
would certainly have been stranded. He would never otherwise
have gained access to theosophical circles.

That is why one should thoroughly study Marie Steiner's situation in the later years, between about 1918 and 1920. I have the
impression that she is no longer at the center of Rudolf Steiner's activity at this time. Rudolf Steiner's efforts in the threefold

social movement were already no longer acceptable to her. In the transcripts of discussions with Waldorf teachers, one can see that she often interrupts him, and this sometimes almost seems like opposition. If one studied her role more closely, one would find that her aims were often quite different from Rudolf Steiner's in these last years. In 1921/22 Steiner gave public lectures and worked with a younger generation that was striving to find new professions. Ita Wegman's era begins then. She is part of Rudolf Steiner's activity after 1922. Perhaps this is a help in gaining a more differentiated view of the riddle of these two women within the anthroposophical movement.

**W W:** Such a down-to-earth account has a healthy effect at least.

**Emanuel Zeylmans:** Yes, I agree. There is a mystery connected with Ita Wegman's life and work, which one must perceive in order to understand the difficulties in the Anthroposophical Society. She was only able to work out of a kind of esoteric enthusiasm. She bore this in her astral body, and it partly permeated her etheric body too. This explains her extraordinary energy and endurance, also after Steiner's death. What I call esoteric enthusiasm was connected with Michael. Sometimes he really lived fully within her, as a few sketches and notes by Rudolf Steiner also testify. When confronted by opposition or opponents she either entered the fray and fought—which dampened her enthusiasm—or she isolated herself. Since she had undergone an esoteric schooling, she did not found a counter-movement or seek to defend herself. But she was therefore no longer influential either.

It is clear that a power from higher worlds lived in Marie Steiner too, but that does not mean she was a heavenly being as an earthly person! Higher beings work through human beings if this can serve human evolution. And I am sure that Rudolf Steiner received help from such heavenly intelligences working through his fellow human beings. Through Marie Steiner he received help connected with the Word (lectures, the Goetheanum building, eurythmy); through Ita Wegman it was more related to deed, to the realization of the esoteric in the outer world. "Doing anthroposophy" was a phrase which Steiner repeatedly used from the 1923 Christmas Foundation Meeting onwards.

Ita Wegman, Rudolf Steiner, and Marie Steiner (Arnheim 1924)

**WW:** On February 27, 1925, Steiner wrote to Marie Steiner: "It is only together with you that I can share judgments of feeling and thought." What does he mean by this, and what relationship does this have to Steiner's collaboration with Wegman?

**Emanuel Zeylmans:** When quoting this, one really ought to include the whole context of the passage where it occurs. People often only quote this one sentence, but reading the whole context gives you a much broader picture. One also needs to remember the situation and point of time when these words were written. It was only a few weeks before Steiner's death and he was writing on his birthday. In this letter he describes his relationship to both women. In writing to Marie Steiner it is very remarkable that he speaks only of thinking and feeling in relation to her, but not willing. In my book I expressed a very extreme perspective on this, which Marie Steiner worshippers cannot accept. But just consider the following—Rudolf Steiner's relationship with Marie Steiner is quite different from that with Ita Wegman and the nature of these relationships changed over time. He also worked intensively with other women as well, such as Edith Maryon. The spirit works through spiritual beings, suprasensory powers, and are connected with people. Steiner even wrote down and sketched the beings in Wegman's case, and actually named them. But I am quite sure that this was also true for individuals like Rosa Mayreder, Pauline Specht, and his first wife Anna Eunike. One cannot say of people—as one can of a rose for instance—that "a person is a person is a person," but one really has to say "a person is a soul is a spirit."

Steiner received help and support from many people. Among them, Alice Sauerwein (circa 1865-1931, General Secretary of the French Anthroposophical Society), Mabel Collins (1851-1927, English theosophist), and Daniel N. Dunlop (1868-1935, General Secretary of the English Anthroposophical Society from 1930 to 1935) who remain more hidden, but were very important to Rudolf Steiner. Something of the world of spirit manifests in every person. One ought not to be too small-minded, but try to think in larger vistas, and then it becomes apparent that he was more connected with Ita Wegman through the will and with Marie Steiner more through thinking and feeling.

### Edith Maryon saved Steiner's life

**W W:** Who was Edith Maryon and what was her relationship to Steiner?

**Emanuel Zeylmans:** Rex Raab, the English architect, published an interesting book about Edith Maryon. A few years previously the Rudolf Steiner estate also published the correspondence between Maryon and Steiner. We therefore have a good picture of the life of this woman who worked in the background. She was the artist who so helped Rudolf Steiner create the statue, the "Representative of Humanity," and did most of the work on it. She worked on this statue in the studio with Steiner for years. She also created the wooden eurythmy figures, which are so useful for eurythmists.

It seems very significant to me that Rudolf Steiner worked with Edith Maryon. She was a reticent person who behaved towards outsiders, above all visitors to the studio, like some kind of Cerberus. She tried to scare everyone away so that Steiner could work in peace. She would have liked to send everyone packing for she knew that Steiner needed time and peace. I myself started to feel a connection with Maryon when I discovered that Steiner wrote verses for her. I compared these poem-like mantras with the verses and mantras he gave Wegman.

**WW:** How do the verses for Maryon and Wegman differ?

**Emanuel Zeylmans:** The verses for Maryon are incredibly profound. The verses for Wegman, which are far more numerous, encompass a whole range of exercises. They also often relate to his relationship with her, or their collaboration. To Maryon, in contrast, he gave descriptions or characterizations from primeval times of human history. For instance Steiner gave her the following verse when she lay ill:

If the gods had only
Consumed themselves in joy,
Never would the world have arisen;
They would merely have dissipated
Their own being into cosmic air:
Sad they grew at this
And lamenting encompassed
Their own being.
And from their lament
The blessed command came forth,
The world-creating Word.

Joy is the fire
That leaps and shines
When lament
Crumbles to ash.

These verses showed me that Edith Maryon must have been an individuality whom Rudolf Steiner addressed as an equal. Someone who receives such thoughts from Rudolf Steiner must have been out of the ordinary. She had probably been a great figure in history.

Edith Maryon

**WW**: Why did Steiner say of her: "She saved my life."?

**Emanuel Zeylmans**: He was working with her on the "Representative of Humanity" and was standing on a ladder. Suddenly he missed his footing. If Edith Maryon had not caught hold of him he would have fallen onto a sharp pole a meter below. Steiner would either have died or have been severely injured at the very least. Maryon saved him by catching hold of him at the right moment. Both of them agreed not to mention this to anyone. But after Edith Maryon died, Steiner described this in his memorial address for her.

### Karma between Edith Maryon and Ita Wegman?

**WW**: In your documentation you quote the following from Ita Wegman's notes:

> 'Some months after the
> fire, the karmic connections
> were revealed to me
> which lay betw. Dr and myself.

—karma had of course
always been between us
The working of karma hindered
by Frl. V. Sivers
" Miss Maryon   <u>India</u>

The inverted commas are probably ditto marks, for in the
handwritten notes they lie directly under the "by" before "Frl. V.
Sivers." What is meant by this hindering of karma through Marie
Steiner and perhaps Edith Maryon also?

**Emanuel Zeylmans:** This note is probably based on an esoteric class, perhaps of May 27, 1923, or one in the autumn of the
same year. I don't know what the note means in relation to Edith
Maryon, though it is certainly strange. When a Dutch person—
and Ita Wegman was Dutch of course—says "Indien," they mean
Indonesia. Indonesia is the former Dutch-Indies. The Dutch refer
to the land that Alexander the Great conquered in sometimes very
bloody campaigns as "India" not "Indien." Perhaps Alexander did
something that resulted in a personal karmic debt connected with
Maryon. But I don't know, for I wasn't able to find out any more
about this.

**WW:** But if Ita Wegman means Indonesia by "Indien," then
it cannot refer to Alexander's karmic debt!

**Emanuel Zeylmans:** Precisely, that wouldn't make sense. For
as far as I know Maryon never had anything to do with Indonesia.
Of course one can speculate wildly. My wife Cordula suspects
that the term "Indien" refers to the fact that both women, Marie
von Sivers and Edith Maryon, were originally more connected
with Indian esotericism. Steiner actually began his more Western
path in 1924, in connection with Ita Wegman.

As I mentioned, Ita Wegman regretted that she came so late to
Rudolf Steiner. When she met him first in 1902 in Berlin, she did
not join his circle. Why did she not become his close colleague
at that time already? She hesitated until 1922. When she was sor-
rowful about this later on, he told her it was indeed a tragic fact,
but that her long reticence had been necessary because she still
had old karma to redeem. She suffered a great deal over this.

It is also possible that the reference to "India" is connected with herself. In any event it is mysterious that the working of karma was supposedly hindered by Maryon and Marie Steiner, for it was Wegman whose karma hindered her from finding a connection to Steiner.

Wegman only met Steiner, by the way, because Steiner had turned towards theosophy. If he had remained a journalist or teacher at the Working Men's College, they would never have encountered one another. This only happened because he became General Secretary of the German Theosophical Society. This enabled her to find him, but at the same time she also met Marie von Sivers. But I cannot say whether she saw and experienced that as a hindrance. In 1912 Maryon came to Dornach. Wegman also could have settled in Dornach or Basel and practised as a doctor, but she didn't do this until 1922. Naturally there are karmic threads linking her and Maryon, but I don't wish to speculate about this.

**W W:** Can one see the fact that Wegman tended Maryon for the sixteen months of her illness as a karmic recompense?

**Emanuel Zeylmans:** She was Maryon's doctor after the latter became seriously ill following the fire on New Year's Eve 1922. An old illness came back to afflict her, which had laid her low between 1910 and 1912. She was continually sick from the night of the fire up to her death in May 1924. This strong-willed, energetic woman who was constantly active on Rudolf Steiner's behalf did not take at all well to her sick-bed imprisonment. She suffered endlessly from having to lie in bed; it was martyrdom for her. Wegman treated Maryon, and Steiner watched very actively over her medical care. In his memorial address for Maryon, Steiner spoke of what he saw as karma working in the fact that Wegman took over Maryon's medical treatment.


### Marie Steiner's breakdown

Until the end of 1922, Maryon was healthy and fully available to Rudolf Steiner. She became ill as a result of the fire, and then Wegman stood ready to serve Steiner.

Marie Steiner had been handicapped by her severe walking disability since 1916. Sometimes she had to be pushed in a wheelchair; she was pushed up the hill in it when the Goetheanum burned down. She had metal leg-braces which helped her walk a little. This disability had its cause in the way experiences affected her—emotional impressions went so deeply into her that they could lead to physical paralysis. Thus it was not a mental but rather a psychosomatic illness. In this respect she was severely ill.

W W: Was her illness caused by anything in this life?

**Emanuel Zeylmans:** It can be traced back to the betrayal by Edouard Schuré, whom she so revered, in 1916. (He turned away from anthroposophy in July 1916, accusing Rudolf Steiner and Marie Steiner of being political activists in favor of the movement for a Greater German [die Alldeutschen]; W W.) Marie Steiner was devastated at this. For three days she lay rigid on her bed and could not move. She had also overworked herself. Thus Rudolf Steiner no longer had someone at his right hand after Maryon fell ill, after the 1922/23 Goetheanum fire—no one who could work actively on his behalf and represent him with a certain degree of knowledge and ability. Of course he had employees and colleagues in his office, but not really anyone at his right hand.

## Rudolf Steiner cried at the graveside

W W: Didn't Wegman write any doctor's notes on Maryon?

**Emanuel Zeylmans:** I don't know. I didn't find any. There is probably a medical dossier, but I wouldn't be able to say anything about it anyway.

**Cordula Zeylmans:** But she worked very hard to help Maryon and kept reporting to Steiner on her state of health.

W W: Why was Steiner so strongly affected by Edith Maryon's death in May 1924?

**Emanuel Zeylmans:** He always expressed himself very openly when close colleagues died. When Christian Morgenstern died (1871-1914), he even cried at the graveside. Margarita Morgenstern told me that his face was streaming with tears. The fact that he felt Maryon's death so strongly shows that he had a deep karmic connection with her. She came from an esoteric background and was member of an esoteric lodge (Golden Dawn) in England.

**WW:** Edith Maryon died on May 2, 1924. In June 1924 Rudolf Steiner was in Koberwitz. From there he sent four letters to Ita Wegman dated May instead of June. How do you explain this error?

**Emanuel Zeylmans:** This mistake is very strange, for all other letters are correctly dated and always written in absolutely calm and composed script. These letters, too, are otherwise without error and give the impression of careful and reflective formulation. They are perfect in form, except for the sole fact that the date is wrong. But I do not know the reason for this. Of course Steiner made errors occasionally in his writing, though very few considering how copiously he wrote.

All that I can imagine is the following. When he wrote to Ita Wegman from Koberwitz he was thinking of something spiritually important that had happened a month before (at the beginning of May). He would have been remembering the circumstances of Maryon's death. In the first volume of my documentation I mentioned the possibility that his mistake might be connected with Maryon's death. Edith Maryon died on May 2 and on May 3 Steiner gave the memorial address. On May 4 and 9 he gave the karma exercises (in GA 236), and on May 6 he gave the funeral address for Maryon. At this time he was working every day with Ita Wegman, in the clinic, and also in the studio. I suspect that very significant exchanges took place between them during this time. These might have been brought about by Maryon's death; Steiner might have told Wegman who Maryon had been in her previous lives. Wegman retained absolute silence about this, although she said that she knew who Maryon had been in former incarnations.

## VI

## SEEKING THE TRUTH —
## THE BIOGRAPHER'S EXPERIENCES

### *Anecdotes as fodder for the sentient soul*

**WW:** Within the anthroposophical movement one meets a
wealth of anecdotes that are often very far from the truth. How
authentic do you think such anecdotes are, and to what extent did
you make use of them in your writing?

**Emanuel Zeylmans:** Working on my book I noticed more
and more that people spoke of Ita Wegman in a confused and
emotional way, and so I decided to base my work exclusively on
historically verifiable facts. Anecdotes are fairly tarnished and
usually try to exert a particular effect. They are often tendentious
and people are blinded by them, forgetting why such tales are
being told and about whom. It is rare that anyone checks up on
where they originated and who is spreading them.

Where there are historical gaps which give rise to questions I
found it best to list such questions in a very meticulous, clearly
formulated way. If one is patient and keeps the questions in one's
mind, the answers always turn up either through a sudden brain-
wave (Intuition) or from without.

The consciousness soul seeks objective truth that is independent of subjective opinion. Even if the truth one discovers is not
what one hoped for, truth comes first. That may be painful—but
that is the nature of the consciousness soul. Properly cultivating
the consciousness soul is usually painful. Anecdotes, in contrast,
are just fodder for the sentient soul. I am interested in rectifying
history, clarifying the truth of what happened. In doing this, as I

said, one also has to live with unanswered questions. The riddle of
Edith Maryon and her relationship to Ita Wegman is such a question. One may even have to live with an unanswered question
throughout one's life, perhaps even through several incarnations.
But I am convinced that an answer will come eventually. Every
true question is answered at some point in the evolution of things.

**WW:** Anna Samweber (1884-1969) circulated many anecdotes about Steiner and his circle, which were then adopted by
other authors. Is there any truth at all in these anecdotes?

**Emanuel Zeylmans:** Anna Samweber is a treasure trove of
anecdotes. She was a housekeeper for Marie Steiner in Berlin.
She could speak especially colorfully about her experiences in
relation to Rudolf Steiner. Jakob Streit, a great reverer of Marie
Steiner, published these tales in book form—so the book *Aus mei-
nem Leben* (From my life) was not written by her at all. In this
booklet, for instance, one finds the anecdote that Marie Steiner
destroyed letters or documents of Steiner's.

And when one also reads in other contexts that important documents, which the Rudolf Steiner estate administration still cites,
were destroyed at some time or other, then it is nothing other than
anecdote. Once a document has been destroyed then the proof
has gone, and it no longer has any value for the objective, con-
sciousness-soul historian. It is a waste of time writing about things
which were supposedly contained in a destroyed document.

There is no real evidence that Marie Steiner destroyed documents, for she kept every little scrap of Steiner's papers. I consider
it simply impossible that Marie Steiner destroyed a letter from
Steiner. I still think it's impossible even if people claim that there
are witnesses who can testify hearing that she had destroyed certain documents. For me, this belongs to the world of fable.

Those who study Rudolf Steiner's relationship to Marie Steiner
as carefully as they can do not need such nonsense. It is obvious
that Steiner could only fulfill his earthly task with Marie Steiner's
help, and that this was determined by destiny. So why do we need
all this letter burning rubbish?

**WW:** What about the supposed diary of Polzer-Hoditz
(1869-1945, active in the threefold social movement among other

---

### *Anna Samweber on the supposed burning of a letter*

"(After the death of Rudolf Steiner) Marie Steiner one day showed me a letter from him in which he wrote that it had been preordained in the world of spirit that he could only fulfill his earthly task together with her. This was one of the very personal letters to her from Rudolf Steiner which Marie Steiner burned. When I asked her why she had done this, saying it would surely have been important for members to know of it, she replied very decidedly: 'But I cannot reveal the most intimate things to this Society!'"

---

things), in which he was said to have written down a conversation he had with Steiner in 1925? This regularly surfaces and is said to be authentic. Where does this falsification come from?

**Emanuel Zeylmans:** From a very active anthroposophical lecturer named Paul Michaelis (1903-1974), who had a very close relationship of trust with Count Polzer-Hoditz in the latter's final years, and who was entrusted with his diaries and all his other notes. I have a declaration by Michaelis in which he claims that he burned a diary of Polzer-Hoditz. This supposedly destroyed diary was said to have contained the most significant statements which Steiner made to Polzer-Hoditz in the last days of his (Steiner's) life—for instance about setting up the second and third classes of the School for Spiritual Science. If he ever said such things it would have been a document of central importance, something one would not destroy.

On February 21, 1968, Paul Michaelis wrote to a former colleague, Erika Warnke: "You ask about Polzer's recollections. I handed them all to the Vorstand four years ago when I thought I would make my way to the clinic." He thought he was going to die. "But I burned all the very private diaries! All of them!" I have this letter, in Michaelis' handwriting.

**W W:** And why did he write this although it was probably a lie?

**Emanuel Zeylmans:** The problem is that one cannot prove that it was a lie. And just as little can one prove that he ever burned anything. But since then people continually quote from what he is supposed to have burned. First of all he spreads all sorts of things which supposedly come from Polzer-Hoditz, and then he burns the documents. It doesn't take a highly developed detective sense to ask the simple question—Why? If he had not "burned" anything, it would have become clear at his death that all of Polzer-Hoditz's notes, etc., were the product of Michaelis' imagination. This is what I will carry on thinking until someone proves the opposite. Whether the things which have been circulated, based on the supposed diary notes of Polzer-Hoditz, are true or not, cannot be ascertained any longer, for there is no evidence to substantiate them.

WW: These purported diaries of Polzer-Hoditz are meant to relate to setting up and leading the second and third class, and to comments about Albert Steffen—including the cynical reference to his supposed incarnation in Mexico?

**Emanuel Zeylmans:** Precisely.

---

### Consciousness soul experiences in researching Ita Wegman's biography

#### An excursus by Emanuel Zeylmans

The consciousness soul consists initially of soul pain. This pain arises when the experience of objective spirit breaks through into one's individual, personal life of soul. The soul then often senses the colossal discrepancy between its own existence and the spirituality of cosmic being, and has the dreadful experience of its individual egotism. A dim awareness arises of the mystery of the ego; and that one's own soul works counter to everything of a divine spiritual nature inasmuch as it does not follow the spirit. The secret of the individual ego is a paradox. If it serves itself it hinders the development of its deepest reality, which consists in devotion to the spirit. If it gives itself up, its individual strength grows and penetrates the soul with spiritual devotion.

But this pain is also an objective cosmic process. The soul warms and illumines like the candle flame consuming its own substance. Thus the pain of the consciousness soul is a fire process that arises between ego and world. If the soul gives itself up to the flame, it finds its higher destiny in this process of destruction—one's own self vanishes. The purpose of the human ego is its higher evolution, beyond individual existence. Goethe formulated this as "To exist we must give up our existence."

By studying history we work at the form which the past assumes in human consciousness. It is a collaboration on the *health of memory*, a therapy for the power of recollection. In an interview with *Die Zeit* on October 29, 1993, Alexander Solshenitzyn described his stance while researching into the February revolution of 1917 in Russia, which he described in his book *The Red Wheel*. He was faced with the fact that a historical account of the revolution had been prevented for seventy years. Former rulers such as Lenin and Stalin created their own mythologies and got rid of uncomfortable witnesses, as well as hiding or even destroying archives. The interviewer objects: "But surely that doesn't mean that a corrected historical picture that later emerges is *necessarily* accurate—it could be just as much a mythology, based on other, different motives." Solshenitzyn replies: "The line dividing good from bad runs through all of us [...] through the heart of each of us." And: "I am open to the idea of using new forms, I'm just against doing it for its own sake."

A later researcher has an advantage over a contemporary witness; it is easier to gain a complete overview. We can also include the motives and impulses of many participating contemporaries in our historical picture, which is why there is only limited value in questioning single "veterans" who were involved at the time. The question of who is in control of our view of history leads ultimately to the question of the integrity of later researchers—their willingness to be objective in the consciousness soul sense—and to their power of intuition. If a historian seeks only the truth and wishes to leave personal will to one side, he or she must continually try to distinguish the essential from the non-essential. To leave aside personal impulses of will, one first has to recognize what these are! In other words, writing history is ultimately also a question of self-knowledge.

It is possible to do this by allowing the theme to guide you; and this in turn is a question of warmth, of devotion to your subject. In other words, you allow your chosen theme to teach you. In the continual willingness to practice self-knowledge you take account of yourself too in your research—objectivity can increase by letting the object of your studies instruct you. Without mixing yourself up in the content of your theme, you nevertheless have to inhabit it fully.

Such methods lead you to thresholds. Research is no longer a personal affair or driven by personal motives. The threshold for me was linked with the experience of thinking. I experienced the fact that the theme I was preoccupied with, the subject of my research, contained ideas which it was my task to perceive. To direct one's whole heart and soul to this, to become wholly an "organ of reception," is the basis for such thinking. I experienced the mystery of thinking—engaging myself unconditionally until the object of my study began to think within me.

It now became difficult to endure the effect of certain texts about Ita Wegman. For instance, the discrepancy between what had emerged as Rudolf Steiner's concern for, and interest in, Ita Wegman and the historical picture that had arisen from the so-called Memorandum. I also found it hard to bear the effect created by Kirchner-Bockholt's book. It was unjust inasmuch as it created a historical picture of former incarnations without addressing the current life. But then the question arises whether I myself have done justice to Wegman in the three volumes of my documented research. And the answer must be: "No!" And yet parts of the mystery have at least become visible as a result.

Next came the question of form, for the consciousness soul requires a harmony between form and subject. The theme itself has a (spiritual) form or shape, and in this case it was particularly agonizing, for one can sense the near impossibility of writing a book about a person like Wegman. Neither a sympathetic, heartfelt book, nor a novel was right in this case. So a chronicle perhaps? But chronicling what? The development of her heart and mind? But little is known of that! So I struggled for ten years—by which time I had reached the age of sixty-three. Then, through meeting Friedmut Kröner, it became possible to realize something of what Rudolf Steiner once described as follows in one of his Esoteric Lessons:

Those who write books whose content is suited as material for meditation must overcome a great temptation. There are books about the highest truths. When we read these a frosty coldness blows towards us, a certain reserve and dryness. And then there are other books which reach out to meet us with warmth of feeling, an overwhelming ardor. Many find these latter enchanting, and prefer them to the former kind of book. And this is the temptation for writers—putting their own feelings, their own enthusiasm, into what they write so as to communicate these to the reader. But how does this affect the reader? If their own feelings are restrained successfully, and only the pure, chaste truth of thinking is presented, which is like a temple, like the pure, chaste Mystery Temple of ancient times, then this pure thinking alone will allow something to light up, kindle within the pupil and lead toward lofty heights of perception and knowledge. But books which are imbued with the writer's own feelings work like consuming fire on the reader and do not allow the reader's own spark to kindle (Berlin, October 29, 1909)

Now of course I am not a teacher as Steiner means it here, but am nevertheless an instrument of the teacher. And thus I was able to find the style suited for my three volumes of research.

I don't want to draw things out too much, and will therefore only tell of the three knotty problems I kept struggling with while working on my books. The first knot was Ita Wegman's relationship with the Anthroposophical Society. She was anything other than a "club person." One simply couldn't see her as the official of a society or association, and I initially found it very difficult to do justice to this theme. But it was this that helped me perceive the wholly new quality of the 1923 Christmas Foundation Meeting. Here Steiner gave (or at least offered) form to a human community which was only distantly related to our traditional view of an association. Everything was wholly and newly based upon what is human. Everything about this new Society, or rather community, calls upon the humanity of its members.

The second knot was Ita Wegman and Marie Steiner. This remained stuck—though I must say that some things related to this question started to move. The biography by Marie Savitch (Dornach 1963) also helps us here. At the moment I do not want to say any more about this. Perhaps this present volume will also help to free this knot a little.

The third problem was connected with the theme of the end of the century. Those who keep an open mind and profoundly strive to understand the relationship between Steiner and Wegman, can sense how one can view Rudolf Steiner's biography from a quite new and different angle. It is as if the meeting with Ita Wegman in 1923 grants him the possibility of grasping a hidden thread once more. Something concealed in Steiner's biography surfaces again at the end of his life and is then writ large—namely, what he has to say about Michael. It is as if a hidden rebirth had occurred between 1900 and 1923, which becomes visible in 1923. Can one call this the birth of Michaelic thinking?

In all events, anthroposophy has now become a matter of deed. Joseph Beuys understood this and expressed it as follows:

> Everything depends
> on warmth
> in thinking —

that is the new quality
of will.

I would only make one possible correction to this—not warmth in thinking, but the warmth of thinking itself. As such I would propose this as a motto for the anthroposophy of the future and for Ita Wegman's relationship to anthroposophy; and thus also for the end of this century and millennium:

Everything depends
on warmth
of thinking —
that is the new quality
of will.

Finally something from Walter Johannes Stein's biography by Johannes Tautz:

Regarding the depiction of history in school lessons, Rudolf Steiner advised that what is often fragmentary knowledge should be inwardly recreated with an exact and active power of imagination, and that one should then allow the result of this to mature until a fully rounded picture arises. "Try to always make whole what is perhaps only incomplete in historical accounts. Complete it in your thoughts. Make every idea concrete, by drawing imagination to your aid, naturally first taking account of all you can learn from history. What you gain from doing this should be carried through sleep; then observe how it has changed. You can certainly present what you have gained in this way to the children." He dismissed my objection that one might easily become inaccurate if one drew on imagination. He said: "After all, you're taking account of everything you can find out, and then you carry through sleep what you have vividly imagined. Then it will really be transformed, for the spiritual world sees to it that truth is revealed. You will

also be able to observe, if you practice this repeatedly
with the same material—for several years in succession
perhaps—that it alters. And it alters so as to become ever
more correct. It will be far more correct than the *fable
convenue* that people call history.

## *Finding a hidden Steiner document*

**WW:** Rudolf Steiner supposedly told Johanna von Keyserlingk (1877-1966) in June 1924 that the Christmas Foundation
Meeting had not been taken up by members; there was still time,
he said, until Michaelmas 1924, but then the demons would
attack. Is this a false anecdote too?

**Emanuel Zeylmans:** This comment was passed on by Rudolf
Meyer (1896-1985, priest of the Christian Community). He was
present at Steiner's "Agricultural Course" at Koberwitz, and was
also a close friend of Johanna von Keyserlingk. Rudolf Meyer
wrote down this comment the moment he had heard it from
Johanna von Keyserlingk. At my request Dr. Gisbert Husemann
verified this with Rudolf Meyer once more in 1980, and saw the
relevant diary entry from 1924. Nevertheless I still had my doubts.
After all, this is a statement by Steiner of very great importance;
and if it is true, I thought, one could better understand his illness. At the end of 1924 he repeatedly spoke to Ita Wegman of
demonic workings, also in the poem "You absurd spell of life,"
which he wrote on his sickbed in November 1924.

In Steiner's *Autobiography: Chapters in the Course of My Life,
1861-1907*, he describes demons as ahrimanic spirits of intoler-
ance, who do not wish to countenance any other possibilities of
thinking. In his karma lectures, on the other hand, he speaks
about the after-death workings of the spirit of Alexander the
Great; of his mission, in fact, to confront and conquer demonic
idols and delusions. Above all these are the delusions of Bacon.

Anyway, for years I doubted the truth of these comments
about demons.

**W W:** Were you ever able to verify this comment by Steiner?

**Emanuel Zeylmans:** Yes and no. My room was already full to bursting with archive material, but in the summer of 1989 I had to go to Arlesheim again. During these weeks there was an unusual heat wave. Strange to say I had the urge to visit the clinic's great archive loft, for on an earlier occasion I had seen a suitcase in a corner there, on which were piled large cardboard boxes. Fortunately I was given permission to look in this suitcase once more, which contained old clinic correspondence. The contents were supposed to have been destroyed, but this hadn't happened yet.

Among these piles of letters I suddenly saw a piece of paper that did not belong there. I pulled it out and immediately saw it was a note by Rudolf Steiner. This piece of paper confirmed what Johanna von Keyserlingk and Rudolf Meyer had said, at least as far as the demons were concerned.

**W W:** How do you regard the fact that you found this piece of paper although you weren't looking for it?

**Emanuel Zeylmans:** If I hadn't found this scrap of writing it would most likely have been burned. However I have frequently experienced such things, and have developed a theory about it. But it is only a theory! A wealth of elemental beings surround every person. I found that Ita Wegman also had some very good ones. One can see that from the fact that she could, for instance, arrive somewhere or other and create order or calm tense situations. Such a thing is possible through the elemental beings one carries around.

According to Steiner various elemental beings have a particularly well-developed intelligence for certain aspects of life. They can perceive in an in-between realm. When one acts instinctively, not quite consciously, they are able to lead one. This is true of very good spirits as well as evil spirits. So I think an elemental being helped me in this search.

### A demon's breakfast

**W W:** The page you found contains the following in Rudolf Steiner's handwriting: "We (the anti-Michael demons) will get

Note sheet by Rudolf Steiner (here rearranged to fit on the page)

through and emerge in the Four if you fail to carry out what is needed by the Michael-Whitsun stroke."

What does this sentence mean?

**Emanuel Zeylmans:** I am not an esotericist and so I cannot be sure. Rudolf Steiner also drew a demon on this page.

**WW:** Is this drawing also on the page that you found in the suitcase?

**Emanuel Zeylmans:** Yes, in fact there is still more—a menu for an English-type breakfast.

**WW:** What does this breakfast consist of?

**Emanuel Zeylmans:** He lists half a roast goose, five eggs, six cups of tea, and a steak. Such food would have been absolute poison for Rudolf Steiner.

**WW:** Is the page dated?

**Emanuel Zeylmans:** No. I suspect that it was about the September 2 or 3, 1924. It also has a humorous quality. When Rudolf Steiner couldn't bear something he used to reproduce it with humor, for instance drawing caricatures.

He also once drew a caricature of Max Kully (1878-1936, Catholic priest at Arlesheim), and this made the latter more bearable for him. Humor or joking is sometimes the only recourse in certain situations. Sometimes it is the only thing that prevents one going under.

**WW:** Wegman and Steiner spoke on many occasions of the various demons that work through people against anthroposophy. For instance Wegman cites Steiner as follows:

In England, he said, he saw Klingsor appearing in the far distance. He did not yet know whether Klingsor had evil intentions; it might also be that the latter did not wish to work against him, but help instead.

In a different article Wegman wrote the following:

These anti-Michael demons, to which Klingsor and his forces belong, were very active and busy, and delivered mocking threats that they would make themselves felt if the Michael impulses that had set to work so powerfully were unable to make headway and break through.

What is meant by these demons?

**Emanuel Zeylmans:** Ita Wegman reported that demons tortured and mocked Rudolf Steiner during his illness. But that was already after Michaelmas 1924. In the preceding period these demons threatened to have their way. They are unfree beings, which is probably characterized in esoteric terms by the phrase "emerging in the Four." I found that in Blavatsky's *The Secret Doctrine*. This means that the demons work through into the visible world. In a painting by Hieronymus Bosch, the *Garden of Earthly Delights*, one can observe these holes in which the demons bore.

## Klingsor

Klingsor's significance in this context is still not clear to me. Klingsor is not a demon but a magician. According to tradition he is "Lord over all demons." He is one of the great magicians, perhaps the very greatest. Replying to a question from Walter Johannes Stein, Steiner once said that Klingsor was a historical individual. We are familiar with him from Wolfram von Eschenbach's Parzival epic. As far as I know, Steiner spoke about him only with great reticence. I do not know why Steiner mentioned Klingsor in England. Klingsor is connected with the Arthurian knights, and Steiner had researched these while in England.

It is also possible that this great magician wished to help Steiner.

**W W:** How?

**Emanuel Zeylmans:** Steiner was a genius at practicing the "accompanying exercises," and thus also at practicing open-mindedness. And why shouldn't the "Lord of all demons" not want to help Rudolf Steiner for once in history? Why not? At least I can imagine this might be possible.

**W W:** This could of course refer to Klingsor's next incarnation, in which, as an individual, he has already released himself from the magic working of his Klingsor incarnation, and therefore wanted to come to Steiner's aid.

**Emanuel Zeylmans:** That is also possible.

**W W:** What relationship does Klingsor have to the anthroposophical movement?

**Emanuel Zeylmans:** Wegman once mentioned in a letter to Walter Johannes Stein that Klingsor has something to do with the Anthroposophical Society. Stein wanted to found a small study circle in Stuttgart to research more deeply into the figure of Klingsor. He was working at the time on his book, *The Ninth Century*, and asked Wegman for advice about Klingsor. She wrote on June 23, 1927:

You can only concern yourself with Klingsor in the company of your very, very best friends, for the threads go deep into the heart of the Anthroposophical Society, and only very few indeed have the possibility of tracing these and seeing how things really stand.

**W W:** And what does she mean by that?

**Emanuel Zeylmans:** I do not know. After a great deal of thought and reflection, I decided not to pursue the theme of Klingsor. One should be very careful indeed when one does not fully understand the spider's web one has woven around oneself.

### The Memorandum has magic influence

Of course I also have to think of the Memorandum in this connection. It was written with enormous intelligence, and has continued since then to exert its obscuring and misleading influence on history. This Memorandum holds great magic sway, for its words are so honed and carefully chosen, and its effect so extraordinarily long-lasting, that it is almost impossible to eradicate its influence from history. Why shouldn't this magic force have a connection with Klingsor? If this were so he would have achieved what he set out to!

**Cordula Zeylmans:** And when your books appeared, the Memorandum started to circulate once more.

**Emanuel Zeylmans:** Quite. When volume one appeared I heard from various friends and acquaintances that the Memorandum had been swiftly delivered to their house to form a basis for their judgement about who Ita Wegman really was.

**W W:** Who started that off?

**Emanuel Zeylmans:** Here, too, silence is the tactful thing.

# VII

# THE CHRISTMAS FOUNDATION SOCIETY

## The Christmas Foundation Meeting

**WW:** I can imagine some people, new to the Anthroposophical Society, attending a few lectures or participating for a while in group meetings. At some point they will certainly hear of the Christmas Foundation Meeting, and they may experience this term as something of a dead weight, without any real content or life. How would you describe the nature of the Christmas Foundation Meeting to them?

**Emanuel Zeylmans:** The Christmas Foundation Meeting took place in Dornach in 1923, and was a congress attended by delegates from all countries of the world in which an Anthroposophical Society or anthroposophical groups were already active. They met together to found an international, all-embracing, worldwide Anthroposophical Society with headquarters in Dornach.

Put like this it was an outer, organizational event. But Rudolf Steiner structured this conference in such a way that this new global Society—in reality a human community for anthroposophy—could become an instrument for him. The Christmas Foundation Meeting was organised in order to supply Rudolf Steiner with a further opportunity for working effectively. In the weeks before the Christmas Foundation Meeting he expressed this very drastically, saying that otherwise he would have to withdraw entirely from the Society.

I see what happened at the Christmas Foundation Meeting entirely from the perspective of Rudolf Steiner's capacity for continuing activity. If one tries to think one's way into the deeds of an initiate like Steiner, one can understand it when he says that the Anthroposophical Society and the anthroposophical movement became one through the Christmas Foundation Meeting.

If one seeks to understand what Steiner means by "anthroposophical movement," particularly when one studies his comments about the reorganisation of the Anthroposophical Society and anthroposophical movement in 1923, then, to put it briefly, it turns out that he is referring to himself when he speaks of the movement. I have also discussed this with others who have come to the same conclusion. Whenever he says that the Anthroposophical Society and anthroposophical movement have become one because he has become chairman, he means himself by the "movement." He was the real bearer of anthroposophy.

This being of the anthroposophical movement thus unites with his outer function as chairman of the Anthroposophical Society. Such union involved an act of profound solemnity. And because the participants at the Christmas Foundation Meeting felt this, in following decades they let it be known throughout the world that an extraordinary mood of reverence and solemnity held sway there. In addition this was the last Christmas shared with Rudolf Steiner, for by Christmas 1924 he was already very ill. The Christmas Foundation Meeting inaugurated the last months of his activity—from then it was exactly forty weeks until he fell ill. In the years following, this gave the Christmas Foundation Meeting a very special aura. In 1944, Marie Steiner published a series of minutes of this Christmas Foundation Meeting, which later became GAs 260 and 260a.

### Steiner was interwoven with anthroposophists' karma

**WW:** Through the Christmas Foundation Meeting Steiner not only bound himself to the destiny of the Anthroposophical Society but also to that of all anthroposophists, in other words to their errors and omissions, too. What does this mean?

**Emanuel Zeylmans:** At the 1923 Christmas Foundation Meeting Steiner also took over chairmanship of the General Anthroposophical Society founded there. In so doing he united

Rudolf Steiner

himself with the deeds of the members of this Society. Whatever any member did or failed to do from then on also affected him as chairman. This is remarkable for two reasons. First, because as an esoteric teacher, he ought not to take any position in an association. He always avoided doing so in the Anthroposophical Society founded in 1913. He was not even a member of the Society, only a kind of honorary president. Second, the new situation rendered him unfree—actually an unthinkable situation for an esoteric teacher. But from then on he allowed himself to be exposed to what his members did, and thus became, in a certain sense, a prisoner of their actions. He was confronted with the very real consequences of his members' actions. This is of course the case for every chairman of an association.

If, for instance, I engage in some kind of anthroposophical nonsense, Manfred Schmidt-Brabant will end up feeling the effect, whether he wishes to or not.

But at the end of 1923 one would not for a moment have imagined how these members would start behaving in subsequent years. At that time people had raised themselves towards an ideal. Only very few members, the quieter ones mostly, already perceived what was brewing below the surface of human relations at Dornach. These brewing soul forces were, however, repeatedly calmed and softened whenever Rudolf Steiner appeared. I am deeply convinced that Rudolf Steiner knew exactly what he was doing when he took over this chairmanship. In 1923/24 one could not have sensed how members would actually start behaving later—but in 1935 emotions bordering on the diabolic break forth in all their horror. One can also see all this in terms of karma. In 1923 Steiner united his destiny so completely with the destiny of the Anthroposophical Society and its members that his future actions came to be partly dictated by this. Through the Christmas Foundation Meeting he interwove himself with members' karma as it was in 1923.

**WW:** As present members of the Anthroposophical Society we too must in some way share in the burden of the Anthroposophical Society's karma—for instance, in all its failures, and in the demons that have been raised. How is it possible for us to live with this?

**Emanuel Zeylmans:** On the one hand the fact that Steiner, by taking on chairmanship of the General Anthroposophical Society, united himself back then with the members—that is, with us too—still has consequences for us today. On the other hand we also help carry all the joys and sufferings of the whole membership. However the joy and the light far outweigh the suffering, for the Christmas Foundation Meeting endowed Steiner with a quite new spiritual dimension and opportunity for effective deed. He gathered around him a small circle, which he called the esoteric Vorstand (or executive committee). This circle of people was intended to protect him; and it was very important to him that Ita Wegman should belong to it. The eight days of the Christmas

Foundation Meeting granted Steiner, as I said, a much more profound relationship to the world of spirit.

## *Intuition about the threefold structure of the General Anthroposophical Society*

**WW:** As a basis for the General Anthroposophical Society, Steiner envisaged a threefold structure—the School as spiritual-scientific institute for teaching and research, the Anthroposophical Society as ideal human association, and the Goetheanum Association (Verein) as the legal body. What was the purpose of this threefold structure?

**Emanuel Zeylmans:** Since I first presented this idea in my Wegman books there has been much discussion about it. In 1985 I saw the threefold structure in this way, and I'm sure that it was reality in the brief period between the Christmas Foundation Meeting and Rudolf Steiner's death. However I do not believe that this threefold structure ought to be the form for the present Anthroposophical Society. I am convinced that this structure is connected with Rudolf Steiner's activity on earth, for it manifests the earthly, organizational form of anthroposophy. That is a difficult concept, which one needs to ponder at leisure.

This idea suggests that a community of spiritually striving people needs a form for its activity. By form I mean the formative force connected with the workings of the exusiae, the spirits of form. The form principle is a very high, form-endowing being necessary for spiritual activity on earth. Steiner once stated:

> It is true that what matters is the spirit of anything and not its form. But just as form without spirit is empty and purposeless, spirit would be ineffectual if it did not create a form for itself.

This is a real meditation, and it leads us straight to the heart of the question of the form of the Anthroposophical Society.

**W W**: You just said that you had *seen* the idea of the Anthroposophical Society's threefold structure. So you did not adopt it from others?

**Emanuel Zeylmans**: People repeatedly claim that this was not my idea. But that is not true. However it is not an idea but a discovery I deduced from Rudolf Steiner's deeds. I made this discovery in 1985. At that time Rudolf Saacke and Gerhard von Beckerath were planning to write a series in *Info3* on the subject of February 8, 1925.

I heard about this because we had links with *Info3*—at the time my wife was a consulting editor. What they were saying made it clear to me that this would be the start of a campaign that would, for a long period, have set rigid, limiting parameters for discussion about February 8, 1925. It was my view that Saacke and Beckerath were spreading chimeras. I am still sure today that the only way to understand the structure of the Anthroposophical Society inaugurated by Steiner is by meditating for years on the Foundation Stone verses and the seven rhythms; and also by including Ita Wegman in the whole thing.

I spent a whole day talking to *Info3* editors to prevent the ideas of Saacke and Beckerath appearing in this magazine as was intended. The discussions grew heated at some points, but it was through them that I gained an intuitive grasp of Rudolf Steiner's ideas and intentions in relation to the Anthroposophical Society's threefold structure.

That was probably the only time in my life that I was aware of having a genuine spiritual intuition. My wife has been meditating on the Foundation Stone verses and the seven rhythms for many years—I have only been doing this consistently since translating my father's booklet. Now I wanted to write everything down for the *Info3* editors. I wrote and wrote, about 80 pages I think. I can still see myself at the moment of receiving this spiritual intuition—I turned to my books and suddenly *saw* Rudolf Steiner's idea. Later on I went through all the many documents with this in mind and saw that it was right!

What I wrote turned into a little pamphlet that I sent to a few people. This calmed the whole situation down somewhat, particularly as far as Gerhard von Beckerath was concerned. Rudolf Saacke also discovered my pamphlet, though not until ten years later, and was enthusiastic enough to want to circulate it internationally.

When my collaboration with Friedmut Kröner began in 1989, he gathered together all the documentation necessary to irrefutably prove Steiner's concept, and wrote everything down in an essay of thirty-five pages. Thus my intuition gained an outer, cast-iron historical basis. This underlay what I published on this theme in my Wegman research, and what Benediktus Hardorp, from his own perspective has recently given full confirmation to in the German anthroposophical newsletter.

But—and I wish to add this here—Saacke, von Beckerath, and Wilfried Heidt helped ensure that the discussion was kept alive. They did not give up, but stuck with this theme for decades. They stayed with it in such a patient and insistent way so that it did not vanish from the earth. Their mountains of paper seem to me like the Letter of St. Jude, verse 9:

> Yet [when] Michael the archangel, contending with the devil, disputed about the body of Moses, he durst not bring against him a railing accusation, but said, The Lord rebuke thee.

In the same way, these three disputed over the threefold corpse of Rudolf Steiner's GAs [Gesamtausgabe; in English: Collected Works (CW)]. They fought with Satan over the dead body of the Society, but they bore this battle patiently.

**W W:** Can you describe this threefold structure in more detail?

**Emanuel Zeylmans:** Three different "limbs" are brought together in the General Anthroposophical Society—The School with individual section leaders; The Association of the Goetheanum of the School for Spiritual Science, also known as the Goetheanum Association (Verein). This was composed of only fifteen voting members and had the legal form of a registered association, administering the Society's property and capital. All other members of this Association were non-voting or contributing members; The Anthroposophical Society founded at Christmas 1923. This united people all over the world who acknowledged the aims of the School for Spiritual Science. Its executive committee, or Vorstand, was called an "initiative" or "esoteric" Vorstand and included Rudolf Steiner (chairman), Marie Steiner (committee member), Albert Steffen (deputy chairman), Ita Wegman (secretary), Elisabeth Vreede (committee member), and Guenther Wachsmuth (treasurer). To this Anthroposophical Society belong all groups of people throughout the world who feel themselves united with anthroposophy. Rudolf Steiner refers to all those people worldwide who concern themselves with anthroposophy as the groups who, through common endeavour, come together to form a spiritual vessel in which anthroposophy can live.

I am summarizing very briefly something that is extremely profound. In my view Steiner also secreted this Society's structure into the Foundation Stone verses as an exercise to be practiced. I see the three calls as follows—"Practice spirit vision" expresses the inner nature of the School; "Practice spirit reflection" is the real task of this new Christmas Foundation Society in developing understanding for each other; and the call of "Practice spirit recollection" is directed towards what remains from before, from old forms. Legal and administrative aspects also include the very highest task of anthroposophy; practising a new way of relating to the external world.

W W: Did the Vorstand hold responsibility for the School?

Emanuel Zeylmans: No. Responsibility for the School cannot lie with the Society's executive committee. A separate School College was formed for that purpose.

W W: Would what was referred to from February 8, 1925 as the Association of the General Anthroposophical Society, in other words the so-called building association, have been able to take over other responsibilities apart from the administration of property and capital?

Emanuel Zeylmans: The fifteen members of this association ought to have offered their function and legal powers to Steiner immediately after the Christmas Foundation Meeting. He waited for this for thirteen long months. If the appropriate arrangements had been implemented, if Steiner had been asked particular questions, then the millions of Swiss Francs—the insurance sum for the First Goetheanum destroyed by fire—could have been used as Steiner intended.

Of course there is no point in speculating what Steiner would have done with this money. But there is a problem connected with it, for insurance sums consist of money which does not derive from people who affirm anthroposophy. At today's rate we are talking, after all, of a sum amounting to between seventy and one hundred million Swiss Francs. From all that I have read of Steiner's views on the nature of money, I am fairly sure that he would not have used this sum for rebuilding the new Goetheanum. I think it is far more likely that he would have put it into other projects that would also have had real relevance for our present times.

**W W:** What kind of things do you mean?

**Emanuel Zeylmans:** In Dornach there was, for instance, no provision whatsoever for the elderly and I can easily imagine that he might, first, have set up a home for all those who needed it. He might also have been able to realize his dream of building a clinic behind the Goetheanum. In my documented research, I published proof that Steiner had planned a clinic on the orchard meadow behind the Goetheanum—a one hundred bed hospital in fact. In other words, he would have transformed the money by using it for another purpose. That is the important thing—to redeem money. This is only one example of how an intrinsically deeply creative person like Rudolf Steiner could have used the money. This would probably have led to quite a new sort of set-up in Dornach, through which he would then have received donations to rebuild the Goetheanum.

### The Christmas Foundation Society's headquarters are in our hearts

**W W:** Now this idea of the threefold structure of the General Anthroposophical Society does not live in most anthropsophists' consciousness. How does the Anthroposophical Society founded at the Christmas Foundation Meeting relate to the Society one can join today?

**Emanuel Zeylmans:** Since Rudolf Steiner's death, or more precisely since February 8, 1925, there are in fact two Anthroposophical Societies. One is called the General Anthroposophical Society, whose headquarters are in Dornach. That is the one you can become a member of. But there is also the other Anthroposophical Society, founded by Rudolf Steiner at the Christmas Foundation Meeting, and the headquarters of this are in our hearts alone. This latter is more spiritually real than the other. It is present wherever a human community cultivates anthroposophy and forms a spiritual vessel for it. It can be present even between two or three people, if gathering on behalf of anthroposophy. Whenever people make efforts on behalf of anthroposophy, this Christmas Foundation Society begins to germinate.

**Cordula Zeylmans:** And anyone who regularly meditates on the Foundation Stone verses contributes something to this human community of the Christmas Foundation Society, by creating spiritual substance for it through meditation. Rudolf Steiner placed himself at the center of this Society, and took over responsibility for it. For me, this deed is essentially a very great spiritual event.

This spiritual Anthroposophical Society can grow and grow through human beings' spiritual striving. But it is very problematic to confuse this latter with the General Anthroposophical Society whose headquarters are in Dornach.

**WW:** I would like to come back for a moment to what you said about form and content. The Christmas Foundation Society is more related to content, that is spirit; while today's General Anthroposophical Society is more related to outer form. But form and content belong together. How do you envisage a harmonious and productive collaboration between the two?

**Emanuel Zeylmans:** I see it differently. I view the Christmas Foundation Society as the real social task—that is of developing social abilities on the basis of an anthroposophical image of the human being. That can only usefully come about when, on the one hand, the activities of the School sections bring spiritual substance to the members; and on the other, when outer necessities function properly—information, co-ordination, organization, finances, buildings, etc. Those are the outer, physical, material things.

Thus one finds in Steiner's concept a reflection of the threefold human being—the School as spirit, the administrative association as physical body, and the Christmas Foundation Society as the soul and arena of social interaction. Each of these three manifests a different relationship between spirit and form.

### The esoteric Vorstand

Rudolf Steiner once commented that the Anthroposophical Society had to be different from what it would have been if he had not assumed chairmanship. After Rudolf Steiner's death Marie Steiner said—and I think this is a striking formulation—that the esoteric Vorstand was "nothing." She said this on April 4, 1925. But one shouldn't forget that this was originally something said by Rudolf Steiner. While he was still alive he said that the esoteric Vorstand was nothing if the members did not accept it.

**WW:** I imagine that not all our readers will know what an esoteric Vorstand means. Can you describe it?

**Emanuel Zeylmans:** It's just a technical term, nothing more. The Anthroposophical Society's only real, worldwide esoteric content came through Rudolf Steiner's activity. The efforts of his pupils made up everything else. But Rudolf Steiner was the only bearer of pure esotericism. It was because he joined this Vorstand that it became esoteric. His relationship to the other Vorstand members of this Christmas Foundation Meeting was esoteric. One cannot understand this with ordinary concepts.

When he set up the School for Spiritual Science Rudolf Steiner nominated individual section leaders and introduced them to members with words such as: "I will lead this field (dramatic and musical arts, together with eurythmy) through its director Frau *Dr. Steiner.*"

Or: "A section will be connected with this which must be especially cultivated because it is a field that, in times when people strove for true spirit knowledge, was always organically, inherently related to such science of the spirit, rather than being just associated with it. It is impossible to consider that what was introduced to humankind as spirit vision, as spirit knowledge in older times, was in any way separate from the study of medicine. And people will come to see from the work which Frau Dr. Wegman is doing with me, and which will shortly be made publicly known, how this synthesis, and even more this organic evolution arises quite naturally through a truly anthroposophical understanding of the world. It is therefore quite natural, in turn, that the medical section will be led through me, with the help of its director Frau *Dr. Wegman.*"

He uses this word "through" in relation to the other section leaders, too. This remained a reality for Ita Wegman after Steiner's death, for he continued to lead the medical section with her help.

**W W**: But seen like that, the Vorstand could still have remained esoteric after Steiner's death!

**Emanuel Zeylmans**: Esotericism stands or falls with inner attitude and approach. And the moment a member of this esoteric Vorstand expresses the view that it is "nothing," it loses its justification. An esoteric community is like a chain—if a link fails, it is a chain no longer.

**W W**: So this community's esotericism dried up because of Marie Steiner's view?

**Emanuel Zeylmans**: Yes. She didn't say this publicly, but wrote it in a letter to Eugen Kolisko. This letter only became known in 1960. Outwardly Marie Steiner continued to go along with the esoteric Vorstand, but one can tell from her behavior that she did not acknowledge it as such. The Vorstand's esoteric quality was extinguished because Marie Steiner had a different view and approach. This attitude of hers interrupted the esoteric nature of the Vorstand.

**W W**: How did she ever come to hold this view?

**Emanuel Zeylmans**: In answering this question it is important to take a careful look at Steiner's relationship to the various members of the Vorstand. If one compares the verses which Steiner gave to Wegman, Maryon, and Marie Steiner, one notices that three quite different kinds of relationships are embodied in them. But each relationship is sustained by profound love and affection towards these three people. Three different qualities exist here. Steiner no doubt had a similar kind of relationship to Steffen, Vreede, and Guenther Wachsmuth. Steiner's relationship to each of these people was incomparably individual. If one tries to understand this, one discovers that every individual can have a totally different relationship to anthroposophy, the Anthroposophical Society, and Rudolf Steiner.

## *The Anthroposophical Society could have had millions of members*

To answer your question one first ought to boldly think through to its conclusion Rudolf Steiner's concept of the Anthroposophical Society, even if this concept was never realized. This concept was heading in the direction of a worldwide Society. If one ponders all of Steiner's comments during the Christmas Foundation Meeting (see GAs 260, 260a and also 259), one sees that the Anthroposophical Society founded in 1923 could have had millions of members. But for this to happen it would have been necessary for the few hundred anthroposophists present at the Christmas Foundation Meeting to have been more open to the world in their forces of soul and spirit.

Indians, African shamans, Buddhists, Muslims, etc. all could have joined this Society. The global character, the international threads that today run everywhere through our civilization, are really Michaelic in character. Steiner calls this cosmopolitan. Then as now people fix their gaze on the few representatives of certain streams within the Anthroposophical Society. In my view that is one of the biggest hindrances which many anthroposophists place in their own path, by going on about these "streams." It is true that Steiner mentioned this a few times in 1923/24, but it should have been laid to rest straight after his death. Anthroposophy is not only for a few streams but for all humankind. And if one wants to become a member of this Anthroposophical Society, one is most heartily welcome. End of story.

**WW**: And one may leave again, of course.

**Emanuel Zeylmans**: Yes, of course. The Christmas Foundation Society ought to be an open Society for all those who see any justification in anthroposophy and in the School for Spiritual Science, and who wish to help sustain it in any way. Anything else has become more and more old-fashioned with the passing years.

**WW**: Assuming we structured the present General Anthroposophical Society according to its earlier form, what would this threefold structure look like, and what actual difference would it make to all anthroposophists?

**Emanuel Zeylmans**: This is an abstract question. Without Rudolf Steiner the Anthroposophical Society is a quite different Society than with him. No one ever gave any thought after Steiner's death to how the General Anthroposophical Society could be newly structured. It would probably have been a good idea to decentralize the world Society immediately after his death, and to found centers in all countries which would have been connected only through international administrative links. The centralized organizational form of the General Anthroposophical Society which we have today only made sense as an esoteric structure during Steiner's lifetime. Decentralization would have also made the international character of the world Society much more apparent.

**WW**: There is a hundred year rhythm for spiritual movements. What significance does this have?

**Emanuel Zeylmans**: It is said that Steiner mentioned this a few times, but I can only tell you what I imagine. In a spiritual movement, non-incarnated people collaborate with incarnated people. Every thirty-three and a third years the impulses of the dead strengthen on earth. If their impulses are not taken up after a hundred years, at the third wave of increased intensity therefore, other spiritual beings appear and make use of the spiritual forms created by the dead. That is how I understand it.

**WW**: Would this apply to the Christian Community as well?

**Emanuel Zeylmans**: Of course, and for all organizations and institutions in which people work spiritually. But in the case of the Christian Community we have to distinguish this clearly from the efficacy of the sacraments. The sacraments are not the same as the *organization* of a religious community, and this hundred year rhythm does not apply to them. They cannot be rendered ineffective by a legal body or religious community, unless of course they are altered.

## Meditating on the Foundation Stone verses

**WW:** What sort of anthroposophical impulses should have been realized by the end of the millennium? What has been achieved and what has not?

**Emanuel Zeylmans:** We have to assume that not everything is visible to us. There is the Michael-prophecy of Steiner's—that certain groups or generations of people should work together at the end of the millennium. In my view people are awakening more and more to this collaborative work. In the anthroposophical movement people are also making ever-increasing efforts to understand one another. Large-scale, visible movements are not necessarily the decisive thing, however. Spiritual deeds carried out in obscurity can be equally significant.

When I say "obscurity" I mean the quiet spiritual practice people cultivate. Don't forget that our knowledge of the Christmas Foundation Meeting is mainly derived from a book that Marie Steiner put together twenty years later (1944), and which, practically unaltered, is still the source people mainly refer to more than half a century later. Now Marie Steiner was not exactly someone who regarded this 1923 Christmas Foundation Meeting as the central focus of Rudolf Steiner's anthroposophy. Biographically she belongs more to the 1902-1920 era, that is the period which I think of as the more Wilhelminian and theosophical one.

**WW:** Wasn't the 1923 Christmas Foundation Meeting the Society's most central event for Marie Steiner?

**Emanuel Zeylmans:** I don't believe so. Look at the correspondence between Rudolf Steiner and his wife, and compare it with the books that were later published about her, *Marie Steiner: Letters and Documents*. Of course this is a very profound question that cannot be answered in a few sentences in an interview. Brief verbal comments might waken old demons again, particularly in this case.

But I will say this: A quite different set of documents could be presented about the Christmas Foundation Meeting than GA 260. The works comprising GAs 260a and 259 are so extensive (altogether about 1,800 pages) that only a few people today can get to grips with them. Historical documents keep growing in volume, and the essence, the spiritual core is easily lost sight of in the process.

**W W:** How do you mean?

**Emanuel Zeylmans:** Well, just take a look at Christoph Lindenberg's booklet on the Christmas Foundation Meeting. Is that really any help to us? And just imagine—that was all that was written in 1993 on the theme of "seventy years of the Christmas Foundation Meeting"—apart from a handful of brilliant essays by Frau Glöckler, designed to dismantle the idea of threefold structure in the General Anthroposophical Society!

**W W:** But how can a person today develop a relationship with the 1923 Christmas Foundation Meeting?

**Emanuel Zeylmans:** By meditating on the Foundation Stone verses and the seven rhythms, and also studying the short addresses Rudolf Steiner gave each day.

**W W:** In other words everything contained in the "special edition" of extracts from GA 260 that Rudolf Steiner Verlag has issued under the title *Die Grundsteinlegung* (Laying the Foundation Stone)?

**Emanuel Zeylmans:** Yes. But this booklet omits the decisive passage where Steiner explains why he is giving the seven rhythms.

**W W:** Where can one find that?

**Emanuel Zeylmans:** On Wednesday, December 26, according to GA 260, Rudolf Steiner interrupted the morning agenda with a short address. In this address he explained the inner reason for giving the seven rhythms. In GA 260 this address covers only

# VIII

# STRUGGLES AND CONFLICTS

*Unredeemed forces from the past must express
and expend themselves*

WW: In the last years of his life Steiner collaborated with Wegman in a particularly intensive way. We can find in the recollections of Oskar Schmiedel (1887-1959, chemist in a medicines laboratory, later to become Weleda) something that Wachsmuth said in a discussion about cultivating esotericism: "The only thing we can do is to link ourselves firmly to Dr. Wegman, for she is currently our only channel to Dr. Steiner."

Is this a reference to what underpinned the close collaboration between Wegman and Steiner?

Emanuel Zeylmans: Through the fact that Wegman consciously linked herself to Steiner he gained new possibilities of cultivating a living esotericism that had great future potential. Steiner himself formulated this in the time after the Christmas Foundation Meeting:

And thus the German theosophical movement entered upon a more theoretical course, as is generally so in the Theosophical Society, and real esotericism had to wait.

And that may perhaps have been a good thing. For three times seven years passed meanwhile, allowing much to enter the unconscious and subconscious that did not really wish to become conscious. And that is what happened. And this means that what could not happen before can begin in a truly esoteric way now, can begin to find its way into the Goetheanistic Christmas impulse, can begin with

Oskar Schmiedel and his wife Thekla in the color laboratory

our search in the karmic realm for esoteric evolutionary impulses in the world, the cosmos and man.

All the esoteric transcripts which the Rudolf Steiner estate has published in several volumes are what Rudolf Steiner refers to as "theoretical esotericism." That may sound strange to people who like reading books, but one should understand that esotericism relates to a mystery of outer things. Novalis expressed this once as follows:

The outer is the inner elevated to a state of mystery.

That is real esotericism! One has to perceive where one's real tasks lie in the outer world. Ita Wegman belongs fully to this view of esotericism.

**WW:** In the above mentioned recollections of Schmiedel we read that Rudolf Steiner never took Marie Steiner with him to the Clinical-Therapeutic Institute, where he worked uninterruptedly with Ita Wegman. Why not?

The Clinical-Therapeutic Institute in Arlesheim

**Emanuel Zeylmans:** I don't know. I only know that Marie Steiner made moral judgements about Ita Wegman. Of course that was very difficult for Rudolf Steiner to bear. That was why, it is said, he invited Ita Wegman to lunch at his house every Sunday, in the hope that the two ladies would be reconciled.

**WW:** But then he could also have taken her with him to the Clinical-Therapeutic Institute now and then.

**Emanuel Zeylmans:** To patient consultations? But there was no reason for Marie Steiner to be there.

**WW:** Is there a connection between the attacks on Wegman and jealousy of her close collaboration with Steiner?

**Emanuel Zeylmans:** Perhaps. Steiner may have been referring to that when he said, on one occasion, that jealousy reared its head if he worked more intensively with one person than with others. But the attacks on Wegman are difficult to understand. I believe they are intimately related to her karma. But of course, as a social-psychological problem within the Anthroposophical Society, the opposition to Wegman remains significant.

**WW:** Schmiedel describes an occasion which highlights the importance of distinguishing the essential from the non-essential. After a dispute with Wegman so fierce that he no longer wished to work with her, he was called to see Steiner. There he gave vehement expression to his criticism of Wegman. Without ignoring the criticism, Steiner did not enter into discussion about what had happened. Instead he presented the essential nature of Wegman to Schmiedel. Perhaps a good deal of the Society conflicts could have been avoided if all the Vorstand members had responded to Wegman in the same way?

**Emanuel Zeylmans:** In another conversation with you, I said that I regard the "accompanying exercises" (Nebenübungen)—thus also this positivity exercise—as among the most esoteric things which Steiner ever gave us, for they relate to mysteries of the outer world. One notices how difficult it is to practice these exercises regularly, but also how enormously effective they are if one succeeds in performing them. One develops the power of distinguishing the true essence of a person from what Rudolf Steiner calls the "undergrowth."

This undergrowth, that we all have around us, is called "astral body" in anthroposophy. Much would be gained if all who have to work together could distinguish an individual and his or her mission from the tangle of undergrowth. Such undergrowth is of course also composed of old, unredeemed karma.

Confronting this soul undergrowth was one of Steiner's greatest difficulties, for there was almost no one in his proximity who did not carry a cloud of unredeemed karma. He never hesitated in bringing this old karma out into the light of day, by putting people through various tests and trials. He knew that unredeemed forces from the past must first express and expend themselves. That was also one of the reasons why I do not just pass negative judgement on all the human struggles and conflicts that took place, for they simply belong to human destiny.

Ita Wegman also possesses such undergrowth of course. She was certainly not a pure Joan of Arc whom the bad world ostracized. These conflicts are a part of her karma. Naturally, she did some wrong and unjust things in previous lives that had to be balanced out in this life. Steiner also mentioned this in a letter to her. I imagine that her past karma expressed and expended itself through all the conflicts with her contemporaries, and thus a balancing out occurred. That is why we shouldn't think only negatively of these conflicts. Of course I know that it is extremely difficult to cope with the Memorandum, and all the minutes and documents, but from this perspective they are texts through which our astral body can practice and learn to endure such conflicts. That's how it was for me, at any rate.

## The shadows of the past

All of them, without exception, were victims of their own egotism, self-deception and self-obsession. Light is only pure where no shadow falls. Even the slightest egotism casts a shadow. That is the destiny of our time and of the earth, for the earth also casts a shadow in the cosmos, a mighty one although we rarely perceive it. Thus all of them without exception were children of the earth. The shadows they cast affect all of us. It is our task to know and perceive so clearly that we never muddle up the shadows we ourselves cast with the shadows of those who preceded us. It is a great task, a bitter task—but necessary and good, for truth is always good.

But our capacity for truth remains stuck in the shadows as long as we fail to discern some beauty in everything that happens on earth, and until we start engendering warmth for the destiny of earth's children, of our predecessors, too.

**WW:** Why is esotericism not a question of the inner but of the outer?

**Emanuel Zeylmans:** "Esotericism" derives from the Greek word meaning inward. In our language it means "secret doctrine" in contrast to exotericism, meaning outward and public. Steiner was always a great opponent of mysticism, of navel-gazing and plunging into your own depths to find the divine there.

Anthroposophy's esotericism is what Goethe calls "an open secret," or, as I mentioned before, what Novalis refers to as "the inner elevated to a state of mystery" in the outer world. The mystery of life does not lie concealed within the human soul, but in the outer events and workings of the world. To put it briefly—the fact that the essence of outer phenomena is hidden from us is not to do with the world but with ourselves. In our conscious awareness we have separated or sundered ourselves from the outer world; and anthroposophical esotericism involves breaking through this barrier of separation. And that means that our senses—seeing, hearing, touching, etc.—must change in such a way that the things of the world can express themselves in us and through us.

GA 245 contains Steiner's exegeses to Mabel Collins' book, *Light on the Path*. He says:

> Reverse your will, strengthen it as much as possible, but do not let it stream out into things as *yours*, but search for the essence of things and then give them your will— allow yourself and your will to stream from things. Let the luminosity of your eyes flow from every flower, every star, but restrain yourself and your tears.

We can see this principle at work in all of Steiner's works throughout his life. Only those who practice this can perceive it there. That is the hidden nature of this open secret, and that is why it is called "esotericism."

### The witch-hunt against Wegman

**WW:** Steiner did not always react to criticism of Wegman as he did towards Schmiedel. He very sharply repudiated others who complained about Wegman to him, so that even Wegman sometimes found it a bit much. Why did he do this?

**Emanuel Zeylmans:** Steiner spoke his mind freely and often expressed himself very fiercely. His outbreaks of anger, though, most probably had pedagogical intent—he used them as he advised Waldorf teachers, too. Many people report that Steiner did this. Perhaps it left a deeper impression. One does not so easily forget such a reaction compared with some comment or other he might have made.

**WW:** Schmiedel also describes Steiner's words during this conversation:

> If the witch-hunt against Frau Dr. Wegman continues, it will lead to the destruction of the Society...And this tendency can also be seen in people who are very close to me. But there, too, I will counter it in the strongest possible way.

Do you think Steiner foresaw the crumbling of the Society into factions?

**Emanuel Zeylmans:** Yes, of course. What became visible to all in 1935 was already present in latent form in 1924. I am certain that Rudolf Steiner knew this. Schmiedel relates this comment to Marie Steiner. That is his opinion, and while he may be right I would regard a "witch-hunt" as something originating in a larger group, so it cannot refer to Marie Steiner's behavior alone.

**WW:** Schmiedel even speaks of Marie Steiner's hatred of Ita Wegman. How did Rudolf Steiner handle that?

**Emanuel Zeylmans:** That too is Schmiedel's point of view, which he must answer for. However I have listened to various older anthroposophists who experienced the last years of Steiner's life. More than one described how Marie Steiner initiated perceptible scenes in which she joined battle with Wegman or expressed very fierce opinions about her. Rudolf Steiner would then try to persuade her to speak more fairly, but she was an emotional personality who could express herself in an unbridled way. But whether Schmiedel is right to call this hatred is another matter—though one shouldn't forget that he himself witnessed these outbreaks.

**WW:** How can one explain the fact that not only Marie Steiner but also her followers pursued Ita Wegman with hatred or at least strong antipathy?

**Emanuel Zeylmans:** I can only explain this through the workings of karma. The old Anthroposophical Society, that wound itself up or became redundant at the Christmas Foundation Meeting, was really something that figured chiefly in German-speaking countries. It was an institution very much connected with Marie Steiner and her followers. The Christmas Foundation Meeting and the School of Michael, on the other hand, had a destiny connection with Ita Wegman.


## The rumor of Steiner's poisoning

**WW:** The rumor that Ita Wegman poisoned Rudolf Steiner keeps circulating. What is the truth of this, and where does this rumor come from?

**Emanuel Zeylmans:** This rumor surfaced while Steiner was still alive. I have encountered it in completely distorted forms, and the fact that it keeps surfacing is due to a psychopath who proclaims it loudly, and has also been circulating it in written form for years. The only helpful response is laughter. As you know I grew up in a clinic where, as my father was a psychiatrist, there were many people suffering from mental illness. They, too, wrote sick fantasies like this psychopath does. One shouldn't let oneself be taken in—just use one's common sense instead.

**WW:** Was Steiner poisoned at all, or is the whole thing a fabrication?

**Emanuel Zeylmans:** It is pure rumor, though in fact caused by something Steiner himself said.

**WW:** This rumor is tenacious and seems to be circulated intentionally. A friend of mine said that a woman told him she was the young eurythmist whom Steiner had staggered up to saying he had been poisoned.

**Emanuel Zeylmans:** Yes, there are a whole lot of reports about this scene. While researching the Wegman book I had to investigate this carefully, and I published the result of my research in the addendum to volume two. Ita Wegman was Rudolf Steiner's personal doctor of course, so I had to find out what she herself said about this. It all fell into place.

One shouldn't forget that the possibility of a criminal attempt to poison Steiner has a colossal, sensational impact, which, once uttered, is impossible to eradicate from history again. Marie Steiner was also quite convinced that poison had played a part. Shortly before her death she said this to an Italian woman, begging her to keep absolutely silent about it, of course. This woman—rather like Anna Samweber—naturally had to go and publish the news immediately. That's how things work. It's pure sensationalism.

I regard the whole affair as a manoeuvre aimed to distract from the real circumstances. In fact the corrupt soul substance of members poisoned Steiner. He could no longer breathe, and it became time for him to leave the earth. This is a form of poisoning which we *should* examine, but of course very few people want to admit such a thing. That is why they distract attention from themselves and transpose an occurrence to a lower level, speaking of physical instead of soul poisoning.

## The time after Steiner's death

**W W:** How did Ita Wegman experience the time immediately after Steiner's death, and how did she come to terms with his death?

**Emanuel Zeylmans:** I have spoken to various people who experienced this, including Ingeborg Goyert, a woman who was twelve at the time and had polio, and was living at the *Sonnenhof* (a curative education institute in Arlesheim). She told me that Ita Wegman came to the *Sonnenhof* on the day of Steiner's cremation, to see that all was in order. She was fit and well and spoke with the children. I heard similar things from others.

After Steiner's cremation she was immediately ready to take up her tasks again, whereas other people were badly thrown, were stunned and confused. Of course Wegman was better prepared than anyone for his death, for she had been at his bedside nearly the whole time. She had been in close proximity with him day and night for almost half a year. As a doctor she was naturally aware of his condition.

On the other hand one has to say that she experienced Steiner's death as a very heavy burden of destiny. Margarete Kirchner-Bockholt once said that for years afterwards Wegman always

The Sonnenhof

withdrew for a few days around the March 30—the day of Stein-er's death—and found things very emotionally difficult during that time. When people talked to her about this she always said that she had come too late to Steiner, and suffered a great deal because of that.

**WW:** Did she continue to feel guided and motivated by Steiner after his death? How did she pursue the path of collabora-tion with him which she had begun?

**Emanuel Zeylmans:** There was an enormously vital force at work in her, and she had received inexpressible gifts and help from Rudolf Steiner. If you take seriously the idea that she had worked together with him in five preceding incarnations then it is understandable that she remained closely connected to him after he died. People who witnessed Ita Wegman in the years after Steiner's death often reported that a great radiance emanated from her, and that she tried in her own way to carry on working as Rudolf Steiner had taught her.

Ita Wegman in Basel (March 1925)

## The "urn dispute" was something else altogether

**WW:** Immediately after Rudolf Steiner's funeral there was an argument between Marie Steiner and Ita Wegman about the urn containing his ashes. What was going on there?

**Emanuel Zeylmans:** There are eleven different versions of this episode. Until Albert Steffen's diary entries and Elisabeth Vreede's notes are published by the people who own these papers, the eleven versions available to me will, unfortunately, continue to provide our only information about this. All eleven come from Marie Steiner's circle, and dramatize this occurrence accordingly. Marie Steiner was someone who belonged culturally to the world of theater, which is why she felt things were only really vivid and alive if they were powerfully dramatized. The "urn dispute" was no exception, and is a story continually brought out and painted in the most varied dramatic hues. Usually it is said that, on April 3, 1925, on the way back from the cremation, Ita Wegman caused deep offence to Marie Steiner with angry and insulting words.

Hagen Biesantz (Vorstand member of the G.A.S. from 1966)
once read out a passage from Elisabeth Vreede's notes on the "urn
dispute" to a larger circle of people. These stated that it had nothing to do with Wegman, but that Marie Steiner had not been able
to bear certain clever and insensitive comments by Albert Steffen. It was Vreede, not Wegman, who then broke out in anger,
against Steffen. The latter had made a tactless comparison with
the quarrel over the body of Thomas Aquinas. That was why
Vreede exploded and snapped at him. There were also apparently
further exchanges of irritation, for everyone was overtired, tense,
and thrown out of balance. The fact that this outbreak of anger
was used as an accusation against Wegman in later years is typical
of the arsenal of weapons employed against her. For even if it were
true, it would only have been an emotional outbreak such as all
were subject to at the time. On several occasions they roared and
bellowed at one another.

**W W:** Why hasn't Biesantz yet published Vreede's notes?

**Emanuel Zeylmans:** I have spoken to him about this a number
of times, but each time he has been fiercely opposed to publication. I would like to express a suspicion of mine that these papers
of Vreede were never meant for him. They come from Elisabeth
Vreede's literary estate, and were intended for the Vorstand of the
General Anthroposophical Society. In other words these papers
were made available to Hagen Biesantz so that the Vorstand might
ponder what is contained in them. But instead he has selected particular literary gems from the notes and circulated them. I suspect
that if all Vreede's notes and reflections were made available, her
accounts would cast a very poor light on the Vorstand that was
in place after Steiner's death. There are probably things there that
Biesantz and others do not want to believe. He is still at liberty to
publish Vreede's notes, or destroy them, or to continue to keep
them as a secret treasure of the "vatican."

**W W:** Are these notes in the care of the whole Vorstand or of
Biesantz alone?

**Emanuel Zeylmans:** They are a matter for Biesantz alone.
These diaries of Vreede we have been speaking of are, he says, at
present stored in his attic.

Ita Wegman in Basel (March 1925)

## The culmination of the conflicts in 1935

**WW:** What were Wegman's official roles between Steiner's death and 1935?

**Emanuel Zeylmans:** Executive committee member of the Association of the General Anthroposophical Society; secretary of this association with right of sole signature; leadership of the fourth sub-section of this association, that is of the clinic; member of the Weleda board of directors; member of the directorate of the School for Spiritual Science; leadership of the medical section of this School; management of the First Class of the School; member of the Vorstand of the Anthroposophical Society from December 1923; secretary of this Vorstand.

**WW:** Why were the five members of the Vorstand after Steiner's death not ready to work together? And why were they not able to do so?

**Emanuel Zeylmans:** Too much was asked of all of them. It was a difficult constellation of members and the changes introduced by the Christmas Foundation Meeting had only just taken place. The people on the Vorstand had very little experience of working together, and enormous contrasts were at work in this small circle.

**WW**: Why did Marie Steiner, Albert Steffen, and Guenther Wachsmuth refuse to work together with Elisabeth Vreede and Ita Wegman?

**Emanuel Zeylmans**: You can't put it like that. The people involved had difficulties with each other. Up until then they had also been engaged in very different sorts of activities. I believe that Vreede couldn't quite cope with Steffen; choleric as she was she perhaps trampled somewhat on his delicate sensibility. And on the other hand Steffen found it hard to endure Wegman—he himself said as much! She also wanted to treat him medically, as he wasn't very well. Thus antipathies developed, and gradually Vorstand meetings ceased!

**WW**: How did Wegman react when Steffen introduced and implemented the idea of continuing to lead the Anthroposophical Society with only three Vorstand members instead of five?

**Emanuel Zeylmans**: Ita Wegman called this the "theft of the Goetheanum."

Roman Boos

**WW:** Roman Boos, in particular, pursued Ita Wegman with a profound hatred. What kind of person was he and what was the reason for his hatred?

**Emanuel Zeylmans:** I have already told you a little about Boos. Robert Friedenthal wrote a short biography of him. Boos was unusually intelligent and was a very educated man; he also carried out some useful research. Due to a severe depressive illness he resigned as Rudolf Steiner's secretary in May 1921. Steiner even forbade him from entering the Goetheanum grounds. He did not reappear in Dornach until after Steiner's death, so he did not experience the years of Steiner's collaboration with Wegman, nor was he present at the Christmas Foundation Meeting in 1923. I don't wish to say any more about Boos. Reading the talks Boos gave between 1926 and 1935, the transcripts of which are recorded in Lilly Kolisko's book, one prefers to take refuge in silence.

# IX

# THE MEMORANDUM AND EXPULSION

## *The Memorandum as cancerous growth*

**WW:** In her article "Aktuelles" (The current situation), Marie Steiner compares emancipation from the Theosophical Society in 1923 with the Anthroposophical Society's liberation from Wegman and Vreede in 1935. Did it not occur to her that in 1913 the anthroposophists were forced out of the Theosophical Society, and that in 1934/35 she and her colleagues were in turn expelling Wegman and Vreede—were therefore assuming the opposite role?

**Emanuel Zeylmans:** If one takes the trouble to read her article carefully, one can only conclude that Marie Steiner must have written this article—which was of some importance to her—in a rather uncontrolled emotional state. I cannot imagine that she would have written it in a calmer, more thoughtful mood, for she would not then have published the embarrassing confusion of thinking that you mention.

**WW:** Are there any signs that Marie Steiner may have previously tried to get Ita Wegman out of the Vorstand and the Anthroposophical Society—perhaps while Steiner was still alive?

**Emanuel Zeylmans:** I am not aware of this. However, as I said before, Marie Steiner remains a riddle to me in many ways. In my view Lilly Kolisko (1889-1976, biologist), presented a very considered judgment about her in the book referred to above. She had a trusting relationship with Marie Steiner and was also valued by her. But we all have a duty to research further into Marie Steiner, for she still remains something of a mystery.

I think that her importance is still greatly overrated, and I experience this as a dreadful injustice towards Marie Steiner herself.

Lilly Kolisko

I believe that it is a great injustice to a person's individuality to so revere and overrate them after their death. Ita Wegman came off better in this respect. Sometimes Marie Steiner worked as a hindering force in the Anthroposophical Society. Such a force is important and may be connected with the karma she shares with Rudolf Steiner. Just by studying the exchange of correspondence between her and Steiner one can see that her significance for anthroposophy is overrated.

**WW:** At the same time Marie Steiner's article appeared in the anthroposophical newsletter, the pamphlet we have often mentioned in this interview also appeared—entitled "Memorandum about matters of concern in the Anthroposophical Society between 1925 and 1935." What is this Memorandum?

**Emanuel Zeylmans:** Those who work through the third volume of my Wegman biography will notice that the Memorandum reprinted there is a text that can exert an insidious effect upon the soul. It was this document that formed people's judgments about Ita Wegman, and was read by the majority of members at the time. After I published my first volume I noticed, as I told you, that certain people had brought back this Memorandum into circulation. That is why, two years later, I felt compelled to republish the whole Memorandum in my third volume.

Every anthroposophist ought to study this Memorandum carefully, for people continually encounter its contents as rumor. It can teach us what an intelligence not directed by human consciousness can think up. I'd like to use a comparison drawn from medicine. This Memorandum is a cancerous growth, a tumor alien to the organism, a product wholly foreign to anthroposophy. Only an intelligence wholly alien to anthroposophy could think up such a piece of work. I do not exclude the possibility that Ahriman is the author of this text. Seen in this light, the Memorandum is wonderful study material, for people who wish to gain insight into the adversary need only read this Memorandum. An experienced anthroposophical doctor thought it advisable to circulate my third volume to all anthroposophical doctors worldwide, so that they might be able to use it to study the influence of anti-human powers, of ahrimanic demons.

## The style of Goebbels

**WW**: What does the Memorandum contain?

**Emanuel Zeylmans**: It is a book, supposedly documenting events, which various people put together to show, at the General Meeting of the General Anthroposophical Society on April 14, 1935, that Ita Wegman was no longer acceptable as a Vorstand member. Although the book was dated February 1935, it did not appear until March of the same year. It was published in a large edition and distributed by the Goetheanum administration. It seems to offer irrefutable proof against Ita Wegman, and also of course against Elisabeth Vreede and six General Secretaries. At the same time it slanders the groups or national Societies connected with these people. The Memorandum gave the impression of being an objective documentation, and it achieved its end, for participants appeared at the General Meeting in large numbers.

The meeting at the Goetheanum was attended by 1,820 people, and I think that most of them had read some or all of this Memorandum, which incited a good deal of indignation at the events of the last ten years.

The Memorandum tries to prove who is at fault, who bears the guilt. I repeatedly studied this work over ten years, mainly during the Whitsun period, until I recognized the mentality that gave rise to it. You can see the hand of Beelzebub in it. Apart from the perfidious deception of its content, this document betrays an ice-cold mockery and scorn. It is the style of Goebbels. The things one cannot accept in oneself are hurled at one's opponent. Basically it has to do with who has key power, in other words power over the buildings, accounts, and membership.

### The accusations against Wegman

**WW:** What were Wegman, Vreede, and the six officials accused of?

**Emanuel Zeylmans:** Basically one can summarize the accusations against Ita Wegman as follows: She intentionally delayed informing Marie Steiner that Rudolf Steiner was close to death, so that the former did not arrive in time; she deeply wounded Marie Steiner with insulting and angry words on the way back from the cremation; she held a session of the First Class in Paris without the knowledge of the Vorstand; she laid claim in a deceptive fashion to authority invested in her by Rudolf Steiner, and also misused her appointment as leader of the medical section and as Vorstand member; her articles in the 1925 newsletter, which she ended six times with "Leading Thoughts," were an attempt to assure and consolidate a particular position of power within the Anthroposophical Society for herself and her followers. She tried to substantiate this position of power by circulating the rumor that she was a reincarnation of Alexander the Great; she began a witch-hunt among her followers against Marie Steiner, disputing Rudolf Steiner's will and trying to get her hands on the former's publishing company. She wanted to build up a power

Ita Wegman (Easter 1927)

base with her followers, and tried to form an Übervorstand (over-Vorstand—a word coined by Marie Steiner) within the Anthroposophical Society; without Marie Steiner's knowledge she had the medical book, *Fundamentals of Therapy*, produced by her publishing company; she falsely claimed that she had co-written this book with Rudolf Steiner, although it was solely by him; in the winter of 1925/26 she had played a decisive part in plans for a World School Association, so as to develop a financial power base within the anthroposophical movement; together with her followers she organized the World Conference in London in 1928, in order to realize her particular international aims and to distract from the opening of the new Goetheanum in Dornach; she had been to blame for getting involved in the disastrous financial affairs of a factory in Einsingen near Ulm, and thus put the General Anthroposophical Society under financial threat and also incurred actual financial damage; without knowledge of the Society executive committee she involved her Arlesheim clinic in financial risks; the international youth camp at Stakenberg had been held by her followers, with her authorization, in a manner that was unworthy of and damaging to the anthroposophical cause; she encouraged the activities of a patient of hers who had paranormal gifts; in 1934 she accepted the Statement of Intent by a number of her followers and thus jeopardized the unity of the Anthroposophical Society; against the will of the Vorstand she acknowledged the Free Working Group in Germany, founded in the summer of 1934, by signing this group's membership cards; she opposed an alteration to the statutes of the Association of the General Anthroposophical Society in 1934 and 1935.

These accusations listed in the Memorandum were once more briefly summarized by Marie Steiner in 1943, after Ita Wegman's death, as betrayal of the spirit of the anthroposophical movement, esoteric mischief, and financial damage to the Society. From other documents one can expand this catalog to include self-deception, striving for sole control, power-lust, bad will, misuse of trust, disloyalty, and dishonesty.

**WW:** Were the accusations justified or were they all completely unfounded?

**Emanuel Zeylmans:** Overall the accusations were not justified. They were problematic inasmuch as there were no witnesses to substantiate most of the accusations. The authors of the Memorandum had not themselves experienced the situations they described. I took the accusations seriously because they seemed very convincing and Ita Wegman did not defend herself at all. The perfidious thing about the situation was that the Memorandum appeared so soon before the General Meeting that those who knew the background to these false accusations hardly had time to react. One cannot refute a whole book in three weeks.

But the Memorandum had the desired effect, for all who were meant to be expelled were indeed expelled from the General Anthroposophical Society. It was only afterwards that people gradually became aware of what had gone on. Willem Zeylmans dictated his response and objection in the summer of 1935. Oskar Schmiedel, who did not belong to the groups around Zeylmans, Dunlop, or von Grone (1887-1978, writer), experienced all the events from close proximity and was so shocked that he could not write his recollections until the time of the Second World War. The only person who reacted immediately with great presence of mind was Polzer-Hoditz. In the three weeks available between publication of the Memorandum and the General Meeting he composed a half-hour talk dissenting from the general view, which he entered on the General Meeting's agenda and then gave there. So he was the only one who offered any resistance at all at this meeting in 1935.

In regard to the accusations themselves, I had to spend months of research before I could discover the actual circumstances. One of the worst accusations, very hard to refute, concerned Ita Wegman's supposed involvement in the business affairs of a button factory in Einsingen near Ulm. My father's literary estate gave me access to fairly precise documents about what had happened at this factory. I also gained additional information from Manfred Schmidt-Brabant and the Wegman archive. I had examine many documents very carefully, until I was able to ascertain, without any doubt, that Ita Wegman did not bear any blame for this factory's financial difficulties. But she had been accused of financially damaging the Anthroposophical Society. It was similar with the other accusations. But we will only be able to form a conclusive opinion about some of them when various people open their archives.

WW: It says in the Memorandum:

> The self-exclusion of the Übervorstand and of two Vorstand members initiated by the Statement of Intent, culminated during the summer of 1934 in the so-called Association of Free Anthroposophical Groups which was founded in complete contravention of the Society's constitution. Such clear enmity to the official leadership of the Society showed that no further reconciliation could be contemplated with those responsible for this association's founding. Apart from the fact that it cannot be recognized by the Vorstand, the founders claim the right to accept people into this association who are not recognized members of the Anthroposophical Society, but whom the founders regard as anthroposophists—with all

the rights normally accorded only to those accepted as members in the proper way. Fräulein Dr.Vreede actually took part in the founding, and has since managed these groups' correspondence, as was announced by Mr. Kaufmann in a circular letter. Frau Dr.Wegman also recognizes and supports this unlawful organization. By so doing, Frau Dr. Wegman and Fräulein Dr.Vreede have in reality excluded themselves from the Vorstand of the Anthroposophical Society.

What is this Statement of Intent?

**Emanuel Zeylmans:** It was founded in 1934 in Germany, Holland, and England. Rudolf Steiner had laid down at the Christmas Foundation Meeting that the people chairing national Societies and groups belonging to the G.A.S. could accept new members; and that the chairman of the Dornach Vorstand would, trusting in these group leaders, confirm this acceptance with his signature. But at the beginning of the thirties Albert Steffen, as G.A.S. chairman, refused to do this any longer. Those who felt they belonged to the Anthroposophical Society, however, then founded this free association. That is exactly what Rudolf Steiner had originally envisaged, for forming groups in this way is a matter of freedom. It is a matter of course for people to be accepted into the Anthroposophical Society who acknowledge the aims of the School for Spiritual Science.

**WW:** What is meant by the "self-exclusion" of Vreede and Wegman from the Vorstand of the Anthroposophical Society?

**Emanuel Zeylmans:** That was an invention of Steffen's, and can be traced back to an old formula in the Roman-Catholic Church, the *Excommunicato ipso facto*. It means that one who publicly rejects particular dogmas of the Church excludes oneself from it by doing so. Steffen introduced this Catholic element into the Anthroposophical Society.

**WW:** Since then one often hears people saying that Vreede and Wegman were not chucked out of the Anthroposophical Society since they "excluded themselves."

**Emanuel Zeylmans:** Exactly. That's how ingeniously things were handled; and today one still hears this view now and then.

Günther Schubert

## *The initiators of the Memorandum*

**W W:** The Memorandum was submitted by twelve gentlemen. But who actually wrote it? Who—if we leave Ahriman to one side—mixed up this poisonous cocktail?

**Emanuel Zeylmans:** Günther Schubert, one of the chief people in the Rudolf Steiner estate office at the time. He wrote and edited it.

**W W:** Did the other eleven also work on it? Were they aware of every detail or did they just sign it?

**Emanuel Zeylmans:** As far as I know—from what I learned from Schmiedel, and Wiesberger's documentation on Marie Steiner—they did not work on this Memorandum, apart from Hermann Poppelbaum (1891-1979, Vorstand member of the G.A.S. from 1949-1966, chairman from 1963-1966). They were just asked to add their signatures.

**W W:** Without knowing what it contained?

**Emanuel Zeylmans:** No, I don't believe so. I'm sure they read it first.

Hermann Poppelbaum

**WW:** Why didn't Albert Steffen, Marie Steiner, and Guenther Wachsmuth sign it?

**Emanuel Zeylmans:** They kept their hands—or rather their names—clean.

**WW:** But it is apparent, surely, that they volunteered ideas for this Memorandum?

**Emanuel Zeylmans:** Of course. They also provided material. During later legal proceedings between the Rudolf Steiner estate administration and the Vorstand it was also said that both Marie Steiner and Albert Steffen had looked through the whole text of the Memorandum and given permission for its publication. The General Anthroposophical Society financed publication, so it wasn't a private initiative on the part of these twelve gentlemen. The book was on public display for a long time on all the Goetheanum's book tables.

**WW:** If Günther Schubert was the author of the Memorandum, how do you explain the fact that several passages in it are largely similar to the November 1934 pamphlet by Poppelbaum, entitled "From the history of the Anthroposophical Society since 1925?" Did Schubert use what Poppelbaum had written or was Poppelbaum the author of the Memorandum after all, or at least its co-author?

**Emanuel Zeylmans:** I published both these texts in my third volume—and you have found passages in the one by Poppelbaum which were transferred almost word for word to the Memorandum. I hadn't noticed that before. I assume that Schubert and Poppelbaum collaborated a good deal, and asked Marie Steiner wherever there were gaps in their story. I suspect that Schubert used Poppelbaum's text as the basis for the Memorandum. My claim that Schubert is the author of the Memorandum is based on a comment by Hella Wiesberger in the book, *Correspondence and Documents: Rudolf Steiner and Marie Steiner.* It says there that Günther Schubert played a decisive role in compiling the Memorandum.

**W W:** In the appendix to his essay "Development and Spiritual Conflict," my father also refers to the author of the Memorandum, but without naming him: "We never hear who the actual author is, but an 'insider' will have no difficulty in recognizing him in almost every line."

## The parting of the ways

We have spoken frequently in our conversation about the reasons for Wegman's and Vreede's expulsion. You have mentioned the issue of "key power" over finances, etc. Was that the real underlying reason for the false accusations used to expel Wegman, or were there are other motives as well?

**Emanuel Zeylmans:** It can happen when people work together in committees that one person starts to find another unbearable. It can get so bad that the very presence of this person, anything he or she says or even doesn't say, becomes unendurable. If you study the book by Lilly Kolisko about the circumstances and conflicts in the Anthroposophical Society up to 1935, you notice that Wegman and Vreede had become unbearable to the other three

Vorstand members. At one of the stormy General Meetings a participant actually cried out that he couldn't bear the fact that Walter Johannes Stein even existed! This seems typical to me of the kinds of feeling that were stirred up.

It's almost a cliché that when things go wrong people head off in different directions—there's a parting of the ways. One party tries to think how the differences can be patched up, while the other seeks someone to blame. After Rudolf Steiner's death things went downhill for the Anthroposophical Society and shared anthroposophical endeavor—there followed ten years of dispute, jealousy, quarrels. Then there was a parting of the ways. The minority—those who were subsequently expelled—wondered how a workable solution might still be found for the problems that had arisen, so that a common path might still be pursued.

### It was always only a question of power

**W W:** How long was the Memorandum officially sanctioned? At what point did the Dornach Vorstand cease circulating it?

**Emanuel Zeylmans:** Not until 1947. But even after that the Dornach Vorstand never officially withdrew it from circulation. No one ever concluded that the content was no longer valid; instead, embarrassingly, the Dornach Vorstand began its conflict with Marie Steiner and her followers. That led, between 1949 and 1952, to a long legal dispute before a Swiss court over Steiner's literary estate. Again, power was the crux of the matter. If one wishes to sum up the mission of the Memorandum in a single word, that word is "power." After Steiner's death Marie Steiner held the power of course. In 1935 it looked as if Albert Steffen would also hold the strings of power, but in the subsequent legal dispute over Steiner's estate she was able to demonstrate that the estate administration office had ultimate power. This tells us something about a person's karma. It was always only a question of power.

**W W:** And money!

**Emanuel Zeylmans:** That's right.

Count Ludwig von Polzer-Hoditz

*He left the Goetheanum in tears after voting against Wegman*

**WW:** Did any of the signatories to the Memorandum retract their signature in later years, and did anyone ever protest publicly about this Memorandum?

**Emanuel Zeylmans:** Three people submitted written protests. The first was Polzer-Hoditz at the 1935 General Meeting. The second was my father, the third, very quietly and unobtrusively, was Oskar Schmiedel. All three documents are reprinted in my third volume. They refute large parts of the Memorandum and the authors underpin their comments with a great deal of material evidence.

None of the signatories ever retracted their signatures. Nor did I ever hear that any of them apologized publicly. But at the lectures I gave on this theme, a few older anthroposophists came up to me and explained why they had voted for Wegman's expulsion at the 1935 General Meeting. Some old, established anthroposophists made very dramatic confessions to me.

**WW**: Can you give an example?

**Emanuel Zeylmans**: Erich Weismann (1905-1984, founder of the Reutlingen Waldorf School) told me that he left the Goetheanum in tears after voting against Wegman. I asked him why he had voted against her in that case. He replied that Albert Steffen had almost forced them into it, for otherwise it would have been a vote by default for his own expulsion. Steffen had threatened to resign if Wegman was not expelled. At that time Albert Steffen exerted a compelling fascination on people, especially at this sort of large General Meeting. His publicly voiced threat, his demand that people choose between these two alternatives, left most members in a fix. The way in which Albert Steffen held sway over these General Meetings, in fact, is a none too glorious a tale.

## *Guenther Wachsmuth and the threefold structure of the G.A.S.*

**WW**: At this General Meeting of the General Anthroposophical Society on Palm Sunday 1935, members present dismissed

Daniel N. Dunlop                    Jürgen von Grone

Eugen Kolisko                    George Adams-Kaufmann

the two Vorstand members Vreede and Wegman, and six officials of the Anthroposophical Society (Daniel N. Dunlop, Jürgen von Grone, Pieter de Haan, Goerge Kaufmann, Eugen Kolisko, Willem Zeylmans) from their posts, or rather expelled them from this Society. Weren't the members of the Association of the General Anthroposophical Society aware that they could not in fact vote on Vorstand members or officials of *another* Society, the Christmas Foundation Society?

**Emanuel Zeylmans:** People often forget that a similar General Meeting had already taken place in 1934, which also aimed to expel Vreede and Wegman. For purely legal, constitutional reasons the expulsion could not be enforced at that time. In 1934, therefore, the course was set, but various people, such as Ernst Marti (1903-1985, doctor), stated that this expulsion was based on a constitutional error. Guenther Wachsmuth made a very emotional reply to this in which he expressed his views about the unified character of the General Anthroposophical Society and the voting rights of its members.

**WW:** One need only take a look at Wachsmuth's book *Die Geburt der Geisteswissenschaft* (The birth of spiritual science), in which he describes Rudolf Steiner's last years, to see, for instance, the strange fact that he makes no mention at all of Ita Wegman's nursing of Steiner in the last year of his life. Instead he describes Steiner's deathbed as though he himself had been there, for instance:

Guenther Wachsmuth

> He folded his hands over his breast, his eyes were firmly, strongly directed towards worlds with which he united himself in vision. As he drew his last breath he closed his eyes himself...

He writes as though he could see through closed doors, as if he had seen it all himself.

**Emanuel Zeylmans:** Wachsmuth is still a rather unknown figure to this day. After his death in 1964, apparently at his direction, all his archives were burned in a large bonfire in his garden. That is why the Dornach Vorstand no longer possesses numerous texts and documents. For example, the official minutes of the founding meeting of August 3, 1924 are missing. He largely erased his own traces. It is also interesting that certain details are now gradually coming to light.

**WW:** Why is so little known about Wachmsuth?

**Emanuel Zeylmans:** I don't think that is quite true. Heinz Herbert Schöffler published a very fine biography of him some years ago. But no one has yet had the courage to examine the forty continuous years of his administration of the General Anthroposophical Society. To do that one would have to include what he published in the newsletter between 1924 and 1964, and be able to plough through the Vorstand archives at the Goetheanum. A figure like Guenther Wachsmuth can only be described against the background of the General Anthroposophical Society between 1924 and 1964, but no one has yet dared do this.

## The emotionally laden General Meeting

**W W:** On April 14, 1935 at the General Meeting, 1,691 members voted in favor of expelling Vreede and Wegman, 76 voted against, and 53 abstained. What sort of state of mind were members in to be able to vote, without further ado, for the expulsion from the Society of two of Steiner's faithful colleagues?

**Emanuel Zeylmans:** I think that such a phenomenon can easily arise whenever a large number of people are crammed together in a relatively small space. Imagine the large hall of the present Goetheanum, which can seat about a thousand people. There were over 1,800 people present at this General Meeting. All the aisles and also the stage were packed with people. Everyone was influenced by the mood of the Memorandum; most people were indignant and aggressive.

As a modern day person, one ought to scrutinize such a phenomenon very carefully. Just think of the mass enthusiasm of young people in German cities at the outbreak of the First World War. People were beside themselves with fervor at being allowed to join up. They set off for war with fiery enthusiasm. That's the kind of situation in which individuals lose self-possession and the power to reflect calmly. The most appalling effects of this mass-suggestion surfaced during the Third Reich. When Hitler spoke to the masses the same thing happened. In Nuremberg, for instance, when the Hitler Youth marched past in serried ranks, this unleashed a quite wild, uncontrolled mood in the watching crowd. I am sure that it is hard to retain one's self-control when one finds oneself in such an emotionally laden crowd of people.

**W W:** So you mean that a kind of mass-suggestion arose at this General Meeting, which obscured people's individual awareness?

**Emanuel Zeylmans:** Yes.

## *All one can do with demons is starve them*

**W W:** Why did Ita Wegman not contest the decision to expel her, against her will, from the Vorstand of the Anthroposophical Society and leadership of the medical section of the School for Spiritual Science?

**Emanuel Zeylmans:** Several times in our conversation I have mentioned that Ita Wegman threw herself into anthroposophy with a kind of spiritual enthusiasm. But the moment she was attacked from without she was defenseless. Her enthusiasm immediately faded at such times. It is true she was capable of fighting back, but she did not do this during the conflicts in the Anthroposophical Society. Madeleine van Deventer said that Steiner had warned Wegman that she should not create any new karma during the rest of her life. One creates such karma by starting to fight and quarrel.

Two people who were present at the General Meetings in 1934 and 1935 told me they asked Ita Wegman why she did not defend herself. Wegman apparently replied that one cannot do battle with demons. Demons, she said, are suprasensible forces, and all one can do is starve them. Of course she did contest the decision to expel her—I documented this—but after her expulsion she did not try to have it revoked. It was probably obvious to her that there was no point.

**W W:** Wegman fell ill when she was expelled from the Anthroposophical Society. Did she have spiritual experiences during this phase?

**Emanuel Zeylmans:** Occasionally this is wrongly reported. The expulsion came on April 14, 1935, following a previous, unsuccessful attempt to do this in March 1934. The internal decision to expel Wegman and Vreede was taken as early as November 1933. In the subsequent period people sought the means to implement this.

**W W:** Did the three other Vorstand members take this decision?

**Emanuel Zeylmans:** Yes. And their adherents of the time as well, of course—above all those from Marie Steiner's circle. We have documentary evidence of this in Günther Schubert's note published (in *Correspondence and Documents: Rudolf Steiner and Marie Steiner*). In the spring of 1934, when Wegman returned from a trip abroad, it became clear to her that she was to be expelled, and then she fell ill. During her illness she kept a diary for the first and last time in her life. As a doctor she recorded the course of her illness. A member of the Rudolf Steiner estate offices, Gian Balastèr, published an article I referred to already, which showed that he had carefully studied my three volumes. He came to the conclusion that Ita Wegman must have undergone a great inner transformation during this illness—though he dates the illness a year late, in 1935.

## The attacks were aimed at Steiner's work

**WW:** Reading Ita Wegman's letters, which she wrote at the time of her expulsion and afterwards, it is astonishing to see how relaxed she is about the slander aimed at her. You already referred to the peaceable and tolerant aspect of her character, and also to the fact that Steiner had instructed her, for karmic reasons, not to hit back with the same kind of vehemence and insults as she received. Wasn't she shocked and indignant at the expulsion?

**Emanuel Zeylmans:** Yes of course she was, deeply shocked and indignant. But she knew all the people well with whom she was in conflict; and I am sure that she could distinguish between the negative forces working through people and the aspects that actually belonged to their individuality. It is often commented that Ita Wegman had an extraordinary ability to deal with the demons working through people. Studying her numerous letters I came to the conclusion that Wegman understood, at the time, that the attacks were only apparently aimed at her, but were really directed at Rudolf Steiner and his work. That, I am sure, is the deeper background to the whole affair. Really there were demonic impulses at work, attacking Rudolf Steiner. These demons continually reared their heads even during his lifetime. Steiner called this "inner opposition."

**Corduma Zeylmans:** Now and then it is claimed that Ita Wegman's character and behavior altered because of spiritual experiences she had after 1935—and this is used to justify accusations against Wegman in the preceding period. However that would be a false conclusion.

**Emanuel Zeylmans:** That is more or less what Balastèr implies; and he goes on to say that if people had been more clear and open about this transformation in Wegman, then Marie Steiner would also have perceived it. He even reproaches me with placing too little emphasis on this supposed transformation of Wegman in my research. So people even blame Wegman for not being forthcoming enough about the fact that she had undergone a transformation!

**WW:** As so often, then, guilt is attributed to the victim. It is remarkable how, in her notebook (number fifty-four), Ita Wegman comments on her own reading of the Memorandum. There she describes the fact that this document does not infuriate her but that she read it with a feeling of great distance, as something wholly alien to her, that was finished and done with. When did she write that?

**Emanuel Zeylmans:** Immediately after the Memorandum had appeared, Wegman wrote in her notebook her views about the accusations raised in it. She started reading with a sense of great apprehension, but as she read she soon saw that the slander really didn't have anything to do with her at all. Wegman's written comments on the Memorandum are a testimony to her objectivity. It took me ten years before I could endure the accusations in the Memorandum with calm composure. Wegman, in contrast, read it immediately after it was published and was clear that the text really only reflected its authors. The Memorandum is a devastating judgement on the authors themselves, and those who allowed it to appear. It had a thoroughly destructive effect on the development of anthroposophical community.

**WW:** Where was Ita Wegman during the 1934 and 1935 General Meetings?

**Emanuel Zeylmans:** In 1934 she was ill and therefore couldn't attend. By the time of the 1935 General Meeting she had long since recovered. While it was going on she worked in the clinic in Arlesheim and tried to counteract the accusations from Dornach by exerting a calming influence on her colleagues. There was clean air in Arlesheim, the Dornach accusations were not discussed in the clinic. Wegman also took great care to ensure that no one spoke badly of Marie Steiner. Such things have no place in a clinic anyway, for a healing atmosphere is needed there.

## A later generation will solve the riddles

Inwardly, in a spiritual sense, all the disputes were far beneath her. She was not only knowledgeable about human beings, but she had also given medical treatment to many of those who later attacked her. This partly occurred while Steiner was still alive, and one can assume with some certainty that Steiner made comments about various people to Wegman in her role as doctor. A true and sovereign superiority dwelt in her. It is true that she gave the impression of being a spontaneous woman, but inwardly a very elevated power lived within her.

At the 1932/33 General Meeting, Roman Boos gave various combative addresses against Ita Wegman, all of which one can read in Lilly Kolisko's book. After one of these General Meetings Wegman returned to Arlesheim with a colleague, who dissolved in tears and expressed her horror at Roman Boos' attack. But Wegman replied: "Don't be upset, Dr. Boos was just finding things very difficult again." Although the attack was directed against Wegman herself, she did not relate it to herself at all.

**W W:** Did she also treat Boos?

**Emanuel Zeylmans:** No, he refused to be treated. Steiner tried to get Boos treated by Wegman. Of course Steiner knew Boos very well, for he was his secretary, Wachsmuth's predecessor.

**W W:** It is certain that demons worked through people in all the conflicts we have been talking about. Yet one shouldn't ignore the individual person in each case, who must still bear responsibility. Couldn't one also see the root of the conflicts in considerable deficiencies of character in those responsible?

**Emanuel Zeylmans:** I used to view these Society conflicts in an extreme light. One of my readers also put forward this kind of extreme point of view in a letter to me, saying that all the conflicts were the battle-ground of spiritual beings, who waged war on one another through the people involved. That is an extreme perspective, which doubtless contains some truth. But something else is also true. If those involved had schooled themselves better, undertaken more self-development, then all the conflicts could have been avoided. That is the opposite, also extreme point of view. There is always something of both in every conflict. For that reason one should explore such circumstances with clear and differentiated judgment.

I have learned to be very careful about judging my contemporaries and historical personalities. For instance, I do not believe that Ita Wegman had either more or less strength of character than Marie Steiner. In my view, therefore, it is not to do with character deficiency, but with people being sucked into a whirlpool of mass judgments. In such situations it is a question of courage, of voicing and standing up for other, different views. At the 1935 General Meeting a mass psychosis occurred.

**WW:** Certainly, but the conflicts and the opposing views about individuals lasted for years. That can't still have been mass psychosis, but was based on individual judgments or rather prejudices. When I spoke of character deficiencies I was referring to the fact that people didn't want to correct these prejudices, or were unable to resolve the conflicts.

**Emanuel Zeylmans:** Yes, we have to see that, and it's certainly another aspect. But I don't believe that current historical writing can describe the events in the Anthroposophical Society between 1924 and 1935 in an objective and comprehensive way. My documentation is only an attempt to make a substantial contribution to this. I hope that in future people will undertake the unrewarding task of carrying out a still more objective and comprehensive account. But to do this the archives have to be opened first. I do not wish to compare the conflicts in the Anthroposophical Society with human conflicts during Nazi rule in Germany. But we have seen how very hard it is subsequently to get a true picture

# X

## THE TIME AFTERWARD

*What would have happened if...*

WW: My next questions are hypothetical, but I'd still like to ask them. Would the conflicts between 1925 and 1935 have taken a different course if people who played a decisive part had practiced the accompanying exercises?

Emanuel Zeylmans: If the five members of the Vorstand had conscientiously practiced the accompanying exercises every day, then, though the difficulties would certainly still have arisen, these would have taken an entirely different course, would have been expressed quite differently. The accompanying exercises go very deep and affect the human being's etheric nature, so that one can develop new capacities after only a few years. They are profound esoteric exercises.

WW: Would the history of the Anthroposophical Society also have been different if Ita Wegman and all the other Vorstand members had worked productively together?

Emanuel Zeylmans: If those in Steiner's immediate environment, above all the other Vorstand members, had practiced inner dying intensively, with all their soul forces, there would have been no reason for Rudolf Steiner to actually die, in outer reality. By inner dying I mean that one overcomes the forces of death present in every human being. Of course egotism does its utmost to avoid passing through this inner death.

Of the five Vorstand members I am of course most familiar with Ita Wegman. If she had succeeded in completely holding herself back, this would have worked wonders! But her Alexandrian urge to conquer did not really fade until after her six-week trip to Greece in 1932. Imagine what effect it would have had if she had been able to overcome this as early as 1925!

**W W:** Would inner opposition also have forced Rudolf Steiner out of the Anthroposophical Society if he had lived longer?

**Emanuel Zeylmans:** An elderly eurythmist, Frau Zondag, died recently in Holland. She had been in Stuttgart from 1922 onwards, and witnessed Rudolf Steiner there in 1923, at the great, tumultuous gatherings in the Anthroposophical Society. She told me how people used to deliver long speeches, and how Rudolf Steiner leaned against the edge of the stage, totally exhausted by having to listen for so long. At one point he called out: "I really have to regard myself as no more than an insignificant presence here." Frau Zondag remembered this moment as one of the most dreadful experiences of her life. At that time, every now and again, Rudolf Steiner was treated like a great but disregarded dignitary. Things would no doubt have continued in that way if Steiner had lived longer. It was Ita Wegman's view that Steiner voluntarily ended his work on earth.

**W W:** Do you also see it like that?

**Emanuel Zeylmans:** I think it's possible. Goethe also believed that people can voluntarily withdraw from life. That is not suicide but an ending of one's activity.

**Cordula Zeylmans:** That's a difficult subject, for at another level Steiner acted right up to his death as though he were going to go on living. My understanding is that he went when the decision came from the world of spirit.

### Affecting world history

**W W:** Do you see any connection between the 1935 General Meeting of the General Anthroposophical Society and the prohibition of the Anthroposophical Society in Germany the same year?

**Emanuel Zeylmans:** Yes and no. I also found this idea in things Wegman wrote, and later noticed that many anthroposophists thought the same. At first I found the idea rather alien. But if you read the lectures which Steiner gave in the last six months of his lecturing activity, the karma lectures above all, then the greatness and historical mission of anthroposophy becomes so mightily apparent that one can indeed conceive of such an idea. Observing our current anthroposophical activity, however, this seems laughable of course. We are no longer a cultural factor at all.

**WW:** But if we take this idea seriously, then anthroposophical activity could be a reflection of contemporary events, or rather the other way round. If we create spiritual forces through spiritual work, these will also affect the outer world. But if a crack or division appears in our shared spiritual endeavor, this would work in the outer world as a destructive force.

**Emanuel Zeylmans:** Of course. But I also consider something else possible. We know from history that the Count of Saint Germain sought out responsible people in political life shortly before the beginning of the French Revolution, and warned them. Walter Johannes Stein also undertook this sort of task and spoke with many politicians. For example he had long talks with Kemal Ataturk in Turkey. These conversations were documented. Stein tried to get Kemal Ataturk to develop new ideas. He also visited King Leopold of Belgium, and in the years before the Second World War was even given an office in his palace. There are addresses by Leopold which Walter Johannes Stein drafted and wrote down for him. Stein also went to London and visited Churchill to get him to develop new ideas. Trying to get Churchill to see things differently was an absolutely hopeless enterprise, but at least he tried. Now just imagine what might have happened if fifty or a hundred anthroposophists had been seized with the same ardor, and, while Steiner was still alive, or shortly after-

Walter Johannes Stein

wards, had tried to exert an influence on world history. I can imagine that this might have achieved something—in a purely outward, not an esoteric way.

## A few weeks before her death Wegman wrote to Marie Steiner

**WW:** Shortly before her death, Ita Wegman wrote a letter to Marie Steiner. Why did she do this although almost all her friends advised her not to?

**Emanuel Zeylmans:** Marie Steiner had published an article in the newsletter; and Madeleine van Deventer told me that she was present when it was shown to Ita Wegman. It appeared in the middle of the Second World War, at Christmas 1942. Marie Steiner's article made an appeal for reconciliation in a current situation that had arisen in Dornach in 1942. But Ita Wegman reflected that Marie Steiner's article might not only refer to the current situation, and consulted with her colleagues because she wanted to reply to it. The former begged her not to make herself look foolish, but she replied: "You with your scepticism ruin everything for me. I am not at all concerned with what Frau Dr. Steiner thinks in her conscious mind, but her words extend a hand towards me, and I would be wrong to ignore it."

After consulting further with the priest Rudolf Meyer, Ita Wegman decided to write to Marie Steiner:

Ascona, February 15, 1943

Dear Frau Dr. Steiner,

Please forgive me for writing to you. I read your article for members in the Goetheanum newsletter, which you wrote shortly before Christmas 1942.

Your article has been interpreted in so many different ways, and I do not allow myself to have a view about it. All I wish to do here is tell you that your words made a deep impression on me. They are great and full of future.

Marie Steiner

Dear Frau Dr. Steiner, please accept my thanks for this.

Yours most truly,

Ita Wegman

She wrote to her without anyone knowing, and sent the letter herself from Ascona. This was a few weeks before her death. Madeleine van Deventer later told me what effect this letter had on Marie Steiner. Van Deventer was a good acquaintance of Rudolf Meyer, who also had close contact with Marie Steiner. Meyer told Deventer that Marie Steiner had Wegman's letter open in front of her when he visited. She showed Meyer the letter and said: "Yet again Wegman has understood nothing." But Ita Wegman died two weeks later, and that struck Marie Steiner like lightning. After all, she was much older, and it was a blow to her that the younger Wegman preceded her into the world of spirit. Rudolf Meyer visited her again after Wegman's death, and this time she had grown very thoughtful.

**W W:** Do we know whether Marie Steiner wished to reply to Ita Wegman's letter?

**Emanuel Zeylmans:** It is said that she did. And once people are dead, one can of course say all sorts of things about them because they can no longer contradict. I think it possible that Marie Steiner wanted to reply to her. And I think it equally possible that this gradually surfaced as anecdote. I myself rely on the *Letters and Documents.* This volume published numerous letters which Marie Steiner wrote after Ita Wegman's death. One needs to study them carefully to find out how Marie Steiner judged Ita Wegman. Even after Wegman's death this judgement was not very edifying. That is why I consider Marie Steiner's supposedly intended answer as rather unlikely.

In the same volume, however, it is also documented that Marie Steiner came to the view, shortly before her death, that the expulsions of 1935 had been a mistake. This was not her idea, though, but came from Ehrenfried Pfeiffer. It was he who recognized that the remaining Anthroposophical Society had gained very little from expelling members.

**W W:** Was Ita Wegman's letter of reconciliation able to balance out some of the accrued karma?

**Emanuel Zeylmans:** You call it a "letter of reconciliation" but is that really how it was intended? These two women had not seen each other for ten years or so. I believe that Wegman only wanted to send Marie Steiner a sign that she had given her article some thought—to remind her, in other words, that she still existed. For I suspect that Marie Steiner only seldom thought about Wegman after 1935. By 1943 Wegman no longer figured for her at all. The Society's newsletter did not even mention Wegman's death. Nor did it refer to Vreede's, six months later.

Yet what Ita Wegman writes to Marie Steiner is very remarkable. Her words "... are great and full of future." If we do not read Marie Steiner's article with the historical context in mind, but as if a deeper substratum of her being had chosen the words, then we can recognize an aspect of Marie Steiner's character that somewhat illumines the riddle of her nature. I can therefore imagine that a working of destiny might be set in motion by the fact that, in a personal letter to Marie Steiner, Wegman used the words "great and full of future" to describe her article.

## Trials and probations

**WW:** In your third volume you write that you regard the conflicts between 1924 and 1935 not only as human failure but also as a precious spiritual treasure. How do you mean this?

**Emanuel Zeylmans:** In the sense that one can see one's own life and that of one's contemporaries as a path of schooling. An elderly person finds it easier to see all of life as a path of self-development. And if you see things like that, you can also reflect on Ita Wegman and the conflicts around her in a more differentiated way.

Despite the work on my three volumes of research, Ita Wegman still remains a conundrum to me in some respects. One cannot deny that her manner infuriated people, and she accordingly came to be treated as a whipping post, a scapegoat—which strikes me as a riddle of history. Did this conceal some kind of trial and probation for Ita Wegman? She was humiliated, mocked, thrown out of the Anthroposophical Society, her most sacred feelings were hurt, the work of Rudolf Steiner, to which she wished to devote her life, was smashed to pieces before her eyes—these are, after all, probations! I personally believe that one should live with such riddles rather than reaching for premature and easy solutions. I have often lain awake and pondered these riddles in great turmoil, have held conversations with Ita Wegman in my thoughts, and always tried to remain optimistic.

What I mean is that we can attain wakefulness through such historical events, that are so difficult to explain. Questions without solutions are good for us—we should endure them and learn to live with them. I am actually thankful that these Society catastrophes occurred—otherwise, perhaps, people might hardly bother to ponder the history of the Anthroposophical Society. In my view it is a matter of great significance to ask what form such a Society should take, for this relates to the problem of community building. Much is written and spoken about this, but very little is attained in this realm—don't you agree Herr Weirauch?

**WW:** Yes indeed.

How did it happen that ten years or so later the rest of the Vorstand collapsed too, and a big chasm opened up between Albert Steffen and Marie Steiner?

**Emanuel Zeylmans:** The period after 1935 was not a happy one for the people in Dornach. They had to some extent isolated themselves by expelling a group of members, and this put human relationships under a great deal of strain. Shortly after this the Anthroposophical Society in Germany was prohibited, and so the largest national Society ceased to exist. The Second World War began four years later. That placed the Swiss Vorstand members in a really dreadful position. The whole world was going up in flames, and in the little haven of Dornach people lived as though cut off from the world. A person who had lived in Arlesheim at the time asked me, after studying my documentation, whether the members expelled in 1935 were not much better off than those who remained in Dornach. The former were free, after all, and could breathe, for they had been released from the weighty chains of Society difficulties.

**Cordula Zeylmans:** There were also many consequences that they no longer had to share in.

**Emanuel Zeylmans:** Without informing Albert Steffen, Marie Steiner founded the Rudolf Steiner estate administration, and offered him no function in it. When this came out there was a huge confrontation, for until then Albert Steffen had quite naturally felt closely involved in the administration of Steiner's literary estate. The dispute began in 1947. There were very many books by Rudolf Steiner in print at the time, but nothing at all like the Gesamtausgabe (The Collected Works of Rudolf Steiner) that we have today. In the archives lay thousands of shorthand transcripts that have not yet been rendered into full-length German manuscripts and published. A real treasure of material. As chairman of the Anthroposophical Society, Albert Steffen felt intimately connected with this, and must therefore have felt deeply wounded when Marie Steiner removed his responsibility for the estate. Above all, this seemed like an unforgivable breaking of trust.

But since she irrevocably pursued her intention, numerous confrontational issues arose that have continued beyond her death. Ultimately they led to legal proceedings between the executive committee of the General Anthroposophical Society and the Rudolf Steiner estate administration. These proceedings were fought out with great ferocity before a Swiss court, and the General Anthroposophical Society lost hands down. The court cited Rudolf Steiner's will as grounds for denying the G.A.S. all claims to copyright of Steiner's works. This opened up a chasm that persisted for decades and divided the different groups from one another. Some absurd things accompanied the split—for instance that Rudolf Steiner's works were no longer sold in the Goetheanum's bookshop.

# XI

# FUTURE PERSPECTIVES

## *Learning from the past for the future*

**WW:** The conflicts we have been speaking about took place fifty to sixty years ago. Almost all the people who were involved have now passed away, and we and the world have continued to develop at a great pace since then. What purpose is there, either now or in the future, in concerning ourselves with these old conflicts between individuals and in the General Anthroposophical Society?

**Emanuel Zeylmans:** I am convinced that one can learn from history. This is also true for one's own biography. Each of us will surely have experienced how certain events or feelings are forgotten and then resurface in our minds a good while later through some small shock or upset. It may be something stupid we did in the past, some mistake or other. It is the same with groups of human beings or idealistic movements. If we really take the activities of anthroposophy in the twentieth-century seriously, as Rudolf Steiner's great work, then we should also take an interest in the history of this impulse. Then one can examine whether the crises and trials suffered in this movement perhaps belong intimately to it.

This is also Rudolf Steiner's approach to world history. In his collected works one finds that he often turns his gaze upon other historical periods, right back to the earliest evolutionary stages of the earth. Rudolf Steiner researched this past and passed on the results of his research to us, and did not spare us descriptions of crises, decline, and fall. That is why, I believe, a time will come when greater distance makes the conflicts in the Anthroposophical Society—which at first sight seem so ugly—appear as part of the struggle for anthroposophy in the twentieth-century. When this future dawns it will be important to be able to reach back to a historical documentation of what happened.

In this I find I am in agreement with Manfred Schmidt-Brabant. In the huge storage spaces of the present Goetheanum, from the cellar to the roof, there are seven different archives—millions of pages of material. He wishes to protect this archive material, believing that it will one day help provide a thorough, extensive biography of the Anthroposophical Society.

**W W:** The shadow side of various individuals and their failures can also help us learn, for our own destiny, how we can carry anthroposophy into the world today, or how we should relate to others in a social context.

**Emanuel Zeylmans:** Precisely, we can learn from them. One thing I learned from them was to focus insults and injuries directed at me in a kind of combustion process and thus endure it.

**W W:** We ought not to forget, either, how we might have acted ourselves if we had been involved in the conflicts in the Anthroposophical Society at the time. Our actions might have been still more extreme! We might have hurt other people much more! Perhaps we would have committed still worse errors!

**Emanuel Zeylmans:** I absolutely agree with you. We can never know how we might have reacted.

**W W:** So it is necessary for anthroposophists today to come to grips with the history of anthroposophy in the twentieth-century in order to use the Society conflicts as a mirror—to see what we need to avoid?

**Emanuel Zeylmans:** Yes. But today psychotherapy is much more advanced in this respect than we anthroposophists. People have recognized that an essential ingredient of modern psychotherapy is learning to look back unwaveringly at one's own difficulties in life, finding the courage to look beyond the veil we draw over uncomfortable events. Then we become able to look at areas of life which profoundly disgust us, but which are directly connected with us. I have always tried to do this, and have noticed how extremely difficult it is. Self-knowledge, observing one's own life objectively, as though from without, is a very arduous and difficult path. The same applies to the anthroposophical movement

and the Anthroposophical Society. The Anthroposophical Society
will only develop and advance when we stop sweeping the conflicts that occurred under the carpet, but instead put them squarely
on the table, spread them out and look at them properly. We have
to be able to endure this. But our Anthroposophical Society hasn't
reached this far yet.

**WW:** What you describe from psychotherapy, observing our
own dark depths, is the encounter with the dragon within—that
is, an encounter with the guardian of the threshold. The same is
true of course for the dark depths of a spiritual or social movement. And if we learn to look into this abyss objectively, it has
a healing effect. But what will happen to the Anthroposophical
Society, or the anthroposophical movement, if we suppress, deny,
or paint a rosy picture of this abyss?

**Emanuel Zeylmans:** I have often pondered this. I see three
great dangers if this happens. First, the substance of anthroposophy will gradually become empty. We may carry on talking about
anthroposophy, but it will no longer have any real effect on life.
Second, anthroposophy will become very trivial and narrow-
minded. One can dilute anthroposophy to such an extent and
alienate it from its true being so that it seems terribly limited—
instead of us ploughing over everything properly and renewing
it. Worst of all is the third danger—that all of anthroposophy
becomes false and insincere, a shabby compromise.

**WW:** Have we anthroposophists of today learned something
from the communication breakdown between the Vorstand
members after Steiner's death? Do you perceive any such learning
process in anthroposophical contexts?

**Emanuel Zeylmans:** Perhaps my views are very idealistic. But
an epoch is already beginning in which one can imagine that a
deeply thoughtful and educated Muslim, a well-read and open-
minded Roman Catholic priest, and perhaps others as well, of
other beliefs, could come together to study anthroposophy. Such
a time will come, and has actually already begun. We shouldn't
lose sight of this perspective. We ourselves tend to live in anthroposophical circles and mix with anthroposophical friends, and
therefore give little thought to this broader, more far-reaching

compass. Rudolf Steiner gave a wonderful foundation for people of different persuasions to connect or converse with one another. In his great work *The Riddles of Philosophy*, he takes a profound look at the ideas of the most important philosophers of the last 2,500 years, and comes to grips with ideas which are often diametrically opposed to his own. If we can see Rudolf Steiner as part of anthroposophy's incarnation on earth, then anthroposophy converses with other worldviews, with quite different approaches. That is a model for us.

## Paths of practice

**WW:** What can the readers of this interview learn from it for their immediate lives?

**Emanuel Zeylmans:** The social aspect. Noticing that we human beings can all learn to practice and develop, to work at things. Rudolf Steiner gave plenty of meditation methods for this, for instance in *The Threshold of the Spiritual World* (CW 17). For me it was a process of learning to become more humble. Actually the anthroposophical movement has fallen into the habit, since Rudolf Steiner's death, of talking very grandly about things sometimes. You only need to look at the catalogs of anthroposophical publishers or at the magazines, to see the ease with which people address the profoundest themes. We ought to try to calm this grand sweep of emotion a little, for we are not all that significant in the world—unfortunately! By making sincere efforts on behalf of anthroposophy, we will find, or at least intensively seek, a personal relationship with Rudolf Steiner. Then belief in authority and the personality-cult type of mood will also disappear.

In addition I can imagine that the speech by the lesser guardian of the threshold from the penultimate chapter of *How to Know Higher Worlds* will become of great importance for many of us. We ought to ponder, sentence by sentence, how the guardian speaks to his pupil. We have mentioned the six accompanying exercises many times. One ought to take prayer very seriously too—

anthroposophists often place less emphasis on this than Rudolf Steiner did. Then we also ought to realize that we pass through the realm of demons each night, and re-enter waking consciousness burdened by them. It is not, I think, generally known in our movement that one can shake off these tatters and shadows in the early morning by meditating when one wakes up.

Then I also learned from Ita Wegman to try to avoid creating new karmic burdens in this present life, for in a subsequent life this binds one to certain conflict situations. This was Rudolf Steiner's great problem—there was hardly anyone around him with a balanced karma. In his lectures *The Fifth Gospel: From the Akashic Record* (CW 148), Steiner describes how Jesus lives on earth for the first time and therefore brings no karma with him. Only thus could he become the bearer of the Christ Being. All human beings should gradually strive in this direction. Many of the strains in the Anthroposophical Society derive from this old, unredeemed karma. I believe we should meet this unredeemed karma with an Eastern attitude, in other words with great calm and composure. I also learned that it is a very good idea to seek a sponsor or mentor among anthroposophists who have died— someone one loves or to whom one feels very drawn.

**WW:** How do you do this in practice?

**Emanuel Zeylmans:** By studying this person's biography. It was this that led Thomas Meyer, for instance, to write the book about Dunlop; and I know people who suddenly discovered Dunlop as a result, and wanted to read everything he wrote. I practiced the same thing with Ita Wegman. She developed into my spiritual mentor. And sometimes she treated me in a very friendly way, protected me too, but above all helped me.

**WW:** Is it enough to read biographies to develop this spiritual mentorship? Shouldn't one also use prayer to establish a relationship with the deceased person, and perhaps ask questions of this individuality in the evening before falling asleep?

**Emanuel Zeylmans:** That is part of it too, of course. One can form a picture of the person and become aware of what others say about him or her. Then one can try, in the evening, to turn one's thoughts towards this person. It is very helpful to think about your spiritual mentor before falling asleep. I have noticed that the things filling one's mind in the evening work on through the night. Then one can find an answer, perhaps, to a question asked the evening before. But if you watch television for several hours at night, read a detective novel, or a newspaper this probably won't happen.

Rudolf Frieling also gave us a good exercise when we were training at the Christian Community's Priest Seminar in Stuttgart. He said: "One should never just take what people say at face value." He meant that we should always test everything with our own powers of common sense, to avoid simply taking over ideas from others without thinking. That was very important for my work on Ita Wegman's biography. It must be possible, therefore, for people to have a quite different view about Ita Wegman than I do, if it is really their own view. You notice immediately when people simply adopt the views of others without thinking, and make them into their own. An anthroposophist ought to practice avoiding this.

W W: The Anthroposophical Society is really a place where people of the most varied kinds can practice working together. If you learn to work together with people you don't in the least feel drawn to, for whom you may even feel antipathy—and nevertheless you work together with them out of free choice—then this spiritual collaboration can give rise to a vessel in which spiritual substance forms. In the past such collaboration broke down, but that itself can become a motivating force for us to gradually realize this ideal, now and in the future.

**Emanuel Zeylmans:** That is a high ideal. Steiner himself was able to do it, for during his lifetime he worked together with everyone, including people he perhaps felt no connection with. This was particularly clear when he joined forces with the theosophists. We can indeed learn to realize such an ideal, by working together with people with whom we have no past ties whatsoever.

### Reactions to the Wegman biography

W W: How did people in the medical section react when your first volume was published?

**Emanuel Zeylmans:** After the first volume appeared Michaela Glöckler published a very positive announcement about it, recommending anthroposophical doctors study it carefully. The second and third volumes also received a recommendation when they were published.

**WW:** What was the reaction of the Rudolf Steiner estate administration?

**Emanuel Zeylmans:** Gratitude, first of all. Hella Wiesberger, to whom I owe a good deal, expressed her admiration after reading the biography, above all at the immense amount of work it involved. She is an expert in this field and can judge such things. Of course some aspects relating to Marie Steiner were hard for her to cope with. I gathered from a few other articles written by people in the Rudolf Steiner estate administration that they did not find this new assessment of Ita Wegman easy to face. The Koberwitz letter of June 11, 1924 had an effect of course—rather like a giant meteorite crashing into a quiet forest lake.

**WW:** How did the Vorstand of the General Anthroposophical Society react?

**Emanuel Zeylmans:** There was no direct reaction from that quarter. However, after the first volume appeared I received a very friendly letter from Jörgen Smit (1916-1991, Vorstand member of the G.A.S. from 1975-1991). When the second and third volumes came out, the Vorstand and the college of the School for Spiritual Science published a long article by Frau Glöckler, in which she rejects the idea of the threefold structure of the Anthroposophical Society. At the time I had to assume that this was the shared view of the Vorstand and School college. The best review of all was written by Klaus Dumke and published in the *Goetheanum* magazine. (see review on page 176)

**WW:** The three volumes of your Wegman biography powerfully redressed the balance by providing a wealth of previously unknown information about Ita Wegman. Did this help in straightening the record and undoing the injustice that had been done to her?

**Emanuel Zeylmans:** It's hard to know if the record has been set straight without, for instance, having a comprehensive biography of

Albert Steffen. One could also, I am quite sure, write a completely different biography of Marie Steiner. With all these individuals from the early years you are faced with the very great problem that their lives are intimately intertwined with the history of the anthroposophical movement. The background must be included, otherwise the author's biography is left hanging in the air. Marie Savitch wrote a wonderful biography of Marie Steiner in 1963, but it has long been out of print.

**WW:** What did the three volumes show today's anthroposophists?

**Emanuel Zeylmans:** Well, certainly that the view of history prevalent in 1990 to 1992 (during which the three volumes appeared) needed a little correction!

---

### Conclusion to Klaus Dumke's review

Putting down the three volumes and asking what their significance is, what their effect is on one's own spiritual position and that of today's Anthroposophical Society—that is, on the position of those friends in spirit both far and near—it once more becomes clear that this is not just a "biography," a literary product. It is not the finished picture of a life, a description that one just lays to one side, and then goes about one's ordinary business again. No, reading these volumes affects one profoundly. Yet the dismay one feels is not personal, but that of an inner contemporary. It is not as if one didn't know a good deal already about what is described here—for instance about the "Society conflicts," about the low point in 1935, and much else besides. It is not that one hasn't always suffered from this. As one reads this documentation, though, which seldom insists on any particular emphasis—in other words, does not try to exert a suggestive influence, what seems to be literary text in fact becomes something else. I believe that this work can become a "shibboleth" [a distinguishing mark – E.Z.] for every single anthroposophist and for the whole Anthroposophical Society. Why? It is my experience that, in the figure of Ita Wegman

> who comes towards us in ever clearer contours in the pages of this documentation, we encounter karmic calling, a lofty spiritual path, but also the tragedy of every spiritual pupil; and ultimately we encounter—as both archetype and reflection—ourselves. We experience a mystery drama. And this makes the encounter more than literature, for it is an existential trial of the individual and the Anthroposophical Society, in relation to the contemporary power of personal karma knowledge and Michael intuition working within them. At the same time it is also a test of the true power of forming community in the sphere of freedom.
>
> (*Das Goetheanum*, August 15, 1993)

I have files full of letters. I have received written reactions from about four hundred people. Some of these letters are quite lengthy. Now and then people tell something from their own life stories, and often relate what they experienced while reading the book. Some of these letters are very interesting indeed. Altogether about five thousand people read the books carefully and conscientiously.

W W: Were you personally attacked after these books came out?

**Emanuel Zeylmans:** Not really. The attacks came before publication. Anyone who has read these three books thoroughly probably no longer has the energy to scold or attack me in writing! It's fairly tiring work to study them. Naturally some anthroposophists were horrified that I published the Koberwitz letter of June 11, 1924.

W W: Is there anything more that should be said that was not contained in the biography?

**Emanuel Zeylmans:** I was very reticent about giving my own opinion in the Wegman documentation. Even in conversation with you I didn't want to speak my mind entirely. I think one or two generations still need to pass before people will dare to openly express the truth about the union between Wegman and Steiner. I don't wish to say any more about it.

## *Looking ahead*

**WW:** Four years have passed since the last volume of your documentation appeared. Looking back now, how do you view the twelve years of work you gave to it? **Emanuel Zeylmans:** I found it very difficult when this work came to an end. I only gradually learned to see that the collaboration between Friedmut Kröner and myself was the fulfilment of old karma rather than the beginning of new collaboration. Once I realized this, I made my peace with the fact that we no longer worked together. I would really so much have liked to start on volume four—a volume of letters with numerous, as yet unpublished treasures. Then I would have liked to continue with volumes five, six, and seven! A volume on esotericism, then one of writings taken from Wegman's literary estate, and finally a book containing all her articles. But even volume two no longer seems precise enough to me. Like volume three it is out of print at the moment. If enough orders arrive in the bookshops we may be able to finance two new editions. But in the meantime I have grown to be seventy years old, and ought to be satisfied that the work

The house at Ersrode

Cordula and Emanuel Zeylmans

has, for the time being, come to completion. But whenever I pick up the volumes, I am always astonished to find how much they contain.

**WW:** What was the significance for you of moving from Reutlingen to Ersrode (near Kassel)?

**Emanuel Zeylmans:** We're now living in the country for the first time, a big change that we like very much. But we also have to adapt. We've met many new people and are glad to live in the middle of Germany, and get to know the East a bit, after living in southern Germany for twenty years. The best of it is meeting people in the neighboring village of Oberellenbach. There's a biodynamic farm and a therapeutic community called Persephone. In Kassel too we have made new contacts.

**WW:** What plans do you have for the remainder of your life?

**Emanuel Zeylmans:** Once you reach seventy, I believe, you can learn to regard each day as an unexpected, rich gift. And in my next incarnation I'd like to be mature much sooner, that is more awake and available for the destiny of the earth. It helps, perhaps, to fill oneself intensely with this wish at the end of one's present life, so that next time everything will be more fruitful.

The things one imbues one's thoughts with now will become active strength in the next life. In this life I wasted a good deal of time with old karma. I'd also like to write poetry, cultivate plants, and work in the garden. And I'd like to try to be as little trouble to my contemporaries as possible.

Lay great thoughts to rest and gather
Yourself in tarrying, come to vision:
What the world desires to build
With you, it only wants to do together.

If the world's to tell you of its scope,
Then wish for what your heart displays to you:
In you must surface what the world found—
Only in your gaze its joy and hope.

(Emanuel Zeylmans)

# BIBLIOGRAPHY

Blavatsky, Helena P.: *The Secret Doctrine: The Synthesis of Science, Religion, and Philosophy.* Pasadena, CA: Theosophical University Press 1997. Originally published in 2 volumes: London, the Theosophical Publishing Company 1888.

Kolisko, Lilly; Kolisko, Eugen: *Ein Lebensbild. Zugleich ein Stuck Geschichte der Anthroposophischen Gesellschaft.* O.O. 1961.

Lehrs, Ernst: *Gelebte Erwartung.* Stuttgart 1979.

Samweber, Anna. *Aus meinen Leben.* Basel 1981.

Savitch, Marie: *Marie Steiner-von Sivers: Fellow worker with Rudolf Steiner.* London: Rudolf Steiner Press, 1967.

Schöffler, Heinz Herbert: *Guenther Wachsmuth — Ein Lebensbild.* Dornach 1995.

Tautz, Johannes: *W. J. Stein. Eine Biographie.* Dornach 1989.

Zeylmans van Emmichoven, J. Emanuel: *Who was Ita Wegman. A Documentation. Vol. 1 – 1876-1925.* Tr. Dorit Winter. Spring Valley, NY: Mercury Press 1995.

———— *Who was Ita Wegman. A Documentation. Vol. 2 – 1925 until 1943.* Tr. Matthew Barton. Spring Valley, NY: Mercury Press 2005.

———— *Who was Ita Wegman. A Documentation. Vol. 3 – 1924 until 1935. Struggles and Conflicts.* Tr. Matthew Barton. Spring Valley, NY: Mercury Press 2005.

Johannes Emanuel Zeylmans van Emmichoven (1926-2008) was born in The Hague. Already in childhood he had close contact with the anthroposophical movement founded by Rudolf Steiner, for his father, the pychiatrist W. Zeylmans van Emmichoven, was the General Secretary of the Anthroposofische Verenigung in Nederland and founder of the Scheveningen Rudolf Steiner Clinic. In 1951, Emanuel Zeylmans started the periodical *Castrum Peregrini* in Amsterdam, which is still in existence today. Then followed years as a bookseller, editor, and publisher. In 1966 he was ordained as a priest in the Christian Community. Between 1968 and 1973 he played a major part in the founding and development of the Dutch periodical *Jonas*.

CPSIA information can be obtained at www.ICGtesting.com
Printed in the USA
BVOW031837190812

298106BV00001BA/6/P